GLENCOE

# PHYSICS

## Principles and Problems

# Lesson Plans

## *GLENCOE*

McGraw-Hill

New York, New York    Columbus, Ohio    Woodland Hills, California    Peoria, Illinois

GLENCOE
# PHYSICS
## Principles and Problems

### Student Edition

### Teacher Wraparound Edition

### Teacher Classroom Resources

Transparency Package with Transparency
  Masters
Laboratory Manual SE and TE
Physics Lab and Pocket Lab Worksheets
Study Guide SE and TE
Chapter Assessment
Tech Prep Applications
Critical Thinking
Reteaching
Enrichment
Physics Skills
Advanced Concepts in Physics
Supplemental Problems
Problems and Solutions Manual
Spanish Resources
Lesson Plans with block scheduling

### Technology

Computer Test Bank (Win/Mac)
MindJogger Videoquizzes
Electronic Teacher Classroom Resources
  (ETCR)
Website at *www.glencoe.com/sec/science*
Physics for the Computer Age CD-ROM
  (Win/Mac)

### The Glencoe Science Professional Development Series

Graphing Calculators in the Science Classroom
Cooperative Learning in the Science Classroom
Alternate Assessment in the Science Classroom
Performance Assessment in the Science
  Classroom
Lab and Safety Skills in the Science Classroom

*Glencoe/McGraw-Hill*

*A Division of The McGraw·Hill Companies*

Send all inquiries to:
Glencoe/McGraw-Hill
936 Eastwind Drive
Westerville, Ohio 43081

ISBN 0-02-825488-0
Printed in the United States of America.

1 2 3 4 5 6 7 8 9  045  05  04  03  02  01  00  99  98

# Contents

## Title                  Page

# To the Teacher

• • • • • • • • • • • • •

The *Physics: Principles and Problems* **Lesson Plans** include complete lesson plans for every numbered section of the textbook. Each lesson plan is geared for the teaching cycle employed in the Teacher Wraparound Edition. The plans are designed for both single-period scheduling and block scheduling. For use in a block schedule, you may wish to follow the suggested activities and resources that are indicated by the 📖 symbol. Refer to "About Block Scheduling" and the Planning Guides for information about curriculum planning for both single-period and block schedules.

Lesson Plans include the following sections:

• **Section Objectives**—lists the objectives found in each section of the student text and the National Science Content Standards for Grades 9–12. Single and block scheduling information is also included.

• **Focus**—provides reference to the Focus Activity included in the *Teacher Wraparound Edition*.

• **Teach**—provides references to all labs and transparencies available in the *Teacher Classroom Resources Package*, plus major teaching opportunities found in the *Student* and *Teacher Wraparound* editions, such as Labs, Pocket Labs, and Demonstrations.

• **Assess/Reteach**—references all Section Review questions in the student text and refers to the Checking for Understanding and Reteaching found in the *Teacher Wraparound Edition*. Also included is the *Study Guide* reference.

• **Enrichment/Application**—includes references to enrichment and extension strategies and materials in the *Teacher Classroom Resources Package* and the *Teacher Wraparound Edition*.

• **Close**—includes references to closure activities in the *Teacher Wraparound Edition*.

• **Chapter Assessment**—found in the last lesson of each chapter and lists references form the Student Edition Chapter Review and the *Chapter Assessment* booklet that can be used to assess student knowledge of chapter concepts. This section also references the *Supplemental Problems* booklet and *Glencoe Science Professional Series*.

• **Multimedia Options**—provides references to the *Science and Technology Videodisc Series* (STVS), *The Mechanical Universe* videotape, *Physics for the Computer Age* and *Interactive Physics* CD-ROMs, Glencoe's *MindJogger Videoquizzes*, and *Computer Test Bank*.

# National Science Content Standards

The National Science Content Standards for Grades 9–12 have been correlated to each section of *Physics: Principles and Problems.* You will find these correlations at the top of every page in this *Lesson Plans* book and on the interleaf pages of the Teacher Wraparound Edition. Correlations are designated according to the numbering system in the table of science content standards shown here.

## Unifying Concepts and Processes
**UCP.1** Systems, order, and organization
**UCP.2** Evidence, models, and explanation
**UCP.3** Change, constancy, and measurement
**UCP.4** Evolution and equilibrium
**UCP.5** Form and function

## Science as Inquiry
**A.1** Abilities necessary to do scientific inquiry
**A.2** Understandings about scientific inquiry

## Physical Science
**B.1** Structure of atoms
**B.2** Structure and properties of matter
**B.3** Chemical reactions
**B.4** Motions and forces
**B.5** Conservation of energy and increase in disorder
**B.6** Interactions of energy and matter

## Life Science
**C.1** The cell
**C.2** Molecular basis of heredity
**C.3** Biological evolution
**C.4** Interdependence of organisms
**C.5** Matter, energy, and organization in living systems

**C.6** Behavior of organisms

## Earth and Space Science
**D.1** Energy in the earth system
**D.2** Geochemical cycles
**D.3** Origin and evolution of the earth system
**D.4** Origin and evolution of the universe

## Science and Technology
**E.1** Abilities of technological design
**E.2** Understandings about science and technology

## Science in Personal and Social Perspectives
**F.1** Personal and community health
**F.2** Population growth
**F.3** Natural Resources
**F.4** Environmental quality
**F.5** Natural and human-induced hazards
**F.6** Science and technology in local, national, and global challenges

## History and Nature of Science
**G.1** Science as a human endeavor
**G.2** Nature of scientific knowledge
**G.3** Historical perspectives

# About Block Scheduling

Single-class and block scheduling each have their own set of advantages and disadvantages. Teachers and schools ultimately choose the option that works better for them. In this section, block scheduling is discussed in greater detail.

To build flexibility into the curriculum, many schools are introducing a block scheduling approach. This type of approach allows curriculum supervisors and teachers to tailor the curriculum to meet students' needs while achieving local and/or state curriculum goals.

Block scheduling can afford many advantages. For students, longer, concentrated periods of study can facilitate the learning of complex material. Furthermore, students may be able to take a wider variety of course work under a block scheduling plan than under a traditional full-year plan, thus enriching their high school experience and giving them a broader foundation of college-level work. Students also benefit by a variety of classroom and instructional experiences—for example, additional student-directed activities and cooperative learning in small groups.

For teachers, the advantages are also balanced with challenges. Block scheduling affords flexibility in your instructional approach, but it also requires extensive up-front planning and imagination. Many teachers are concerned with how to fill 90-minute periods. You may begin class by having students work in pairs on a student-directed activity for 10–15 minutes. The next 10–15 minutes may be teacher directed, followed by 10 minutes of a second student-directed activity, 20 minutes of instruction, and closing with a third student-directed activity. Clearly, this plan requires creative arrangements and plans.

Block scheduling also affords teachers the opportunity to explore interdisciplinary activities. For example, with a 90-minute block, you might collect data for 45 minutes and have a math teacher perform and explain the mathematical analysis of the data for the remaining 45 minutes. You might work with teachers to incorporate other subjects. Again, these arrangements require commitment from and consensus among teachers, curriculum supervisors, and so forth.

If you follow a block schedule, you may want to consider either combining lessons or eliminating certain topics and spending more time on the topics you do cover. **Physics: Principles and Problems** provides the flexibility that allows you to tailor the program to your needs. **Physics: Principles and Problems** also provides a variety of support materials in the *Teacher Classroom Resources* that will help you and your students, whether you follow a block schedule or single-class schedule.

In the planning guides that follow, it is assumed that for block scheduling, the course will be taught for one semester and include 90 periods of approximately 90 minutes each.

Please remember that planning guides are provided as aids in planning the best course for your students. Use the planning guide that relates to your curriculum and the ability levels of the classes you teach, the materials available for activities, and the time allotted for teaching. The planning guide will assist you in developing and following a schedule that will enable you to complete your goals for the school year or semester.

# Planning Guides for *Physics: Principles and Problems*

| Chapter/Section | Single-Class (180 days) | Block (90 days) |
|---|---|---|
| **The Science of Matter and Energy** | | |
| **1    What is physics?** | **1** | **1** |
| Physics: The Search for Understanding | 1/2 | 1/2 |
| Chapter Review | 1/2 | 1/2 |
| **2    A Mathematical Toolkit** | **6** | **3 1/2** |
| 2.1   The Measures of Science | 1 | 1/2 |
| 2.2   Measurement Uncertainties | 2 | 1 1/2 |
| 2.3   Visualizing Data | 2 | 1 |
| Chapter Review | 1 | 1/2 |
| **Mechanics** | | |
| **3    Describing Motion** | **6** | **3 1/2** |
| 3.1   Picturing Motion | 2 | 1 |
| 3.2   Where and When? | 1 | 1/2 |
| 3.3   Velocity and Acceleration | 2 | 1 1/2 |
| Chapter Review | 1 | 1/2 |
| **4    Vector Addition** | **6** | **4** |
| 4.1   Properties of Vectors | 2 | 1 1/2 |
| 4.2   Components of Vectors | 3 | 2 |
| Chapter Review | 1 | 1/2 |
| **5    A Mathematical Model of Motion** | **8** | **5** |
| 5.1   Graphing Motion in One Dimension | 1 | 1 |
| 5.2   Graphing Velocity in One Dimension | 2 | 1 1/2 |
| 5.3   Acceleration | 2 | 1 |
| 5.4   Free Fall | 2 | 1 |
| Chapter Review | 1 | 1/2 |
| **6    Forces** | **8** | **4 1/2** |
| 6.1   Force and Motion | 2 | 1 |
| 6.2   Using Newton's Laws | 3 | 2 |
| 6.3   Interaction Forces | 2 | 1 |
| Chapter Review | 1 | 1/2 |
| **7    Forces and Motion in Two Dimensions** | **8** | **4 1/2** |
| 7.1   Forces in Two Dimensions | 2 | 1 |
| 7.2   Projectile Motion | 3 | 2 |
| 7.3   Circular Motion | 2 | 1 |
| Chapter Review | 1 | 1/2 |

**KEY**
*SE* = Student Edition, *TWE* = Teacher Wraparound Edition, *TCR* = Teacher Classroom Resources, *STVS* = Science and Technology Videodisc Series, *PCA* = Physics for the Computer Age

# 1 Lesson Plans

## Physics: The Search for Understanding

### Section Objectives

_____ **Define** *physics*.
_____ **Relate** theory, experiment, and applications to the role they play in physics research.
_____ **Demonstrate** that, while there is no single scientific method, there are common methods used by all scientists.

**National Science Content Standards** UCP.1, UCP 2, UCP 3; A.1, A.2, D.3, D.4, E.1, E.2, F.1, F.6, G.1, G.2, G.3

**Schedule**
Block schedule: 1 session
Single-period schedule: 1 session

### Focus

_____ Discrepant Event, *TWE* p. 4

### Teach

_____ Pocket Lab, *SE* p. 5
_____ Music Connection, *SE* p. 6
_____ Physics & Society, *SE* p. 8
_____ Help Wanted, *SE* p. 9
_____ Physics Lab, *SE* p. 12
_____ Quick Demos, *TWE* pp. 3, 5
_____ Tech Prep, *TWE* p. 6
_____ Demonstration 1–1, *TWE* pp. 6–7

_____ Applying Physics, *TWE* p. 9
_____ Physics Journal, *TWE* p. 9
_____ *Laboratory Manual, Lab 1.1, TCR*
_____ Transparency 1 Master and Worksheet, pp. 1–2, *TCR*
_____ *Physics Lab and Pocket Lab Worksheets, pp. 1–3, TCR*
_____ *Spanish Resources, TCR*

### Assess/Reteach

_____ Checking for Understanding, *TWE* p. 10
_____ Reteaching, *TWE* p. 11

_____ *Study Guide, pp. 1–6, TCR*
_____ *Reteaching, pp. 1–2, TCR*

### Enrichment/Application

_____ Cultural Diversity, *TWE* p. 5
_____ Enrichment, *TWE* p. 6
_____ Connections to Mathematics, *TWE* p. 10

_____ Extension, *TWE* p. 11
_____ *Critical Thinking, p. 1, TCR*
_____ *Enrichment, p. 1, TCR*

### Close

_____ Closing Strategy, *TWE* p. 11

### Chapter Assessment

_____ Chapter Review, *SE* p. 13
_____ Assessment, *TWE* p. 7
_____ *Chapter Assessment, pp. 1–4, TCR*

_____ *Alternate Assessment in the Science Classroom*
_____ *Performance Assessment in the Science Classroom*

### Multimedia Options

_____ **Videodisc:** *STVS* Physics, Disc 1, Side 2, Ch. 3; Chemistry, Disc 2, Side 1, Ch. 16; Earth & Space, Disc 3, Side 1, Ch. 13
_____ **CD-ROM:** Introduction; What Is Physics?, *PCA*

_____ **Videotape:** *MindJogger Videoquizzes*
_____ **Videotape:** *The Mechanical Universe*, Quads 3, 4
_____ **Software:** *Computer Test Bank*

# 2.1 Lesson Plans

## The Measures of Science

### Section Objectives

_____ **Define** the SI standards of measurement.
_____ **Use** common metric prefixes.
_____ **Estimate** measurements and solutions to problems.
_____ **Perform** arithmetic operations using scientific notation.

**National Science Content Standards** UCP.1, UCP.3; A.1, E.1, E.2, G.1, G.3

**Schedule**
Block schedule: 1/2 session
Single-period schedule: 1 session

### Focus

▢ Discrepant Event, *TWE* p. 16

### Teach

_____ History Connection, *SE* p. 18
▢ Pocket Lab, *SE* p. 19
_____ Using a Calculator, *SE* p. 23
▢ Quick Demos, *TWE* pp. 15, 17
_____ Applying Physics, *TWE* p. 18
_____ Tech Prep, *TWE* p. 19

▢ Demonstration 2–1, *TWE* pp. 20–21
▢ Transparency 2 Master and Worksheet, pp. 3–4, *TCR*
▢ *Physics Lab and Pocket Lab Worksheets*, p. 7, *TCR*
_____ *Spanish Resources, TCR*

### Assess/Reteach

▢ Section Review, *SE* p. 23
_____ Checking for Understanding, *TWE* p. 22
▢ Reteaching, *TWE* p. 23

▢ *Study Guide*, pp. 7–9, *TCR*
_____ *Supplemental Problems, TCR*

### Enrichment/Application

▢ Extension, *TWE* p. 23
_____ Cultural Diversity, *TWE* p. 17

_____ *Critical Thinking*, pp. 2–3, *TCR*

### Close

▢ Activity, *TWE* p. 23

### Chapter Assessment

_____ *Alternate Assessment in the Science Classroom*
_____ *Performance Assessment in the Science Classroom*

### Multimedia Options

▢ **Videotape:** *MindJogger Videoquizzes*
▢ **Videodisc:** *STVS* Physics, Disc 1, Side 2, Ch. 3

_____ **Software:** *Computer Test Bank*

# 2.2 Lesson Plans

## Measurement Uncertainties

### Section Objectives

_____ **Distinguish** between accuracy and precision.
_____ **Indicate** the precision of measured quantities with significant digits.
_____ **Perform** arithmetic operations with significant digits.

**National Science Content Standards:** UCP.1, UCP. 2, UCP. 3; A.1, A.2, E.1, E.2, G.2

**Schedule**
Block schedule: 1 1/2 sessions
Single-period schedule: 2 sessions

### Focus

_____ Discrepant Event, *TWE* p. 24

### Teach

_____ Help Wanted, *SE* p. 26
_____ Quick Demo, *TWE* p. 25
_____ Applying Physics, *TWE* p. 25
_____ Physics Journal, *TWE* p. 27
_____ *Laboratory Manual*, Labs 2.1, 2.2, TCR

_____ *Physics Skills, Skills 1–13, TCR*
_____ *Graphing Calculators in the Science Classroom*
_____ *Spanish Resources, TCR*

### Assess/Reteach

_____ Section Review, *SE* p. 29
_____ Checking for Understanding, *TWE* p. 28
_____ Reteaching, *TWE* p. 29

_____ *Study Guide*, pp. 10–11, TCR
_____ *Supplemental Problems, TCR*

### Enrichment/Application

_____ Extension, *TWE* p. 29

_____ *Tech Prep Applications*, pp. 1–4, TCR

### Close

_____ Cooperative Learning, *TWE* p. 29

### Chapter Assessment

_____ Assessment, *TWE* p. 26
_____ *Alternate Assessment in the Science Classroom*

_____ *Performance Assessment in the Science Classroom*

### Multimedia Options

_____ **Videotape:** *MindJogger Videoquizzes*
_____ **Videodisc:** *STVS* Physics, Disc 1, Side 2, Ch. 12

_____ **Software:** *Computer Test Bank*

# 2.3 Lesson Plans

**KEY**
SE = Student Edition, TWE = Teacher Wraparound Edition, TCR = Teacher Classroom Resources, STVS = Science and Technology Videodisc Series, PCA = Physics for the Computer Age

## Visualizing Data

### Section Objectives

_____ Graph the relationship between independent and dependent variables.

_____ Recognize linear and direct relationships and interpret the slope of a curve.

_____ Recognize quadratic and inverse relationships.

**National Science Content Standards** UCP.1, UCP.2, UCP.3; A.1, A.2, E.1, F.6

**Schedule**

Block schedule: 1 1/2 sessions

Single-period schedule: 3 sessions

### Focus

_____ Focus Strategy, TWE p. 30

### Teach

_____ Pocket Lab, SE p. 31

_____ Design Your Own Physics Lab, SE p. 32

_____ How It Works, SE p. 35

_____ Physics Journal, TWE p. 31

_____ Quick Demo, TWE p. 33

_____ Connections to Chemistry, TWE p. 33

_____ Demonstration 2-2, TWE pp. 34-35

_____ Physics Lab and Pocket Lab Worksheets, pp. 5-6, 8, TCR

_____ Spanish Resources, TCR

### Assess/Reteach

_____ Section Review, SE p. 36

_____ Checking for Understanding, TWE p. 36

_____ Reteaching, TWE p. 36

_____ Study Guide, p. 12, TCR

_____ Reteaching, p. 3, TCR

_____ Supplemental Problems, TCR

### Enrichment/Application

_____ Extension, TWE p. 36

_____ Enrichment, pp. 3-4, TCR

### Close

_____ Cooperative Activity, TWE p. 36

### Chapter Assessment

_____ Chapter Review, SE pp. 37-41

_____ Assessment, TWE p. 33

_____ Chapter Assessment, pp. 5-8, TCR

_____ Alternate Assessment in the Science Classroom

_____ Performance Assessment in the Science Classroom

### Multimedia Options

_____ CD-ROM: Tools, What Is Physics?, Mathematical Relationships, PCA

_____ Videotape: MindJogger Videoquizzes

_____ Videodisc: STVS Physics, Disc 1, Side 2, Ch. 16

_____ Software: Computer Test Bank

# 3.1 Lesson Plans

## Picturing Motion

### Section Objectives

_____ **Draw** and **use** motion diagrams to describe motion.

_____ **Use** a particle model to represent a moving object.

**National Science Content Standards** UCP.1, UCP.2, UCP.3; A.1, A.2, B.4

**Schedule**

Block schedule: 1 session

Single-period schedule: 2 sessions

### Focus

_____ Activity, *TWE* p. 44

### Teach

_____ Help Wanted, *SE* p. 46

_____ Quick Demos, *TWE* pp. 43, 45

_____ Physics Journal, *TWE* p. 45

_____ Transparency 3 Master and Worksheet, pp. 5–7, *TCR*

_____ *Laboratory Manual*, Lab 3.1, *TCR*

_____ *Spanish Resources*, *TCR*

### Assess/Reteach

_____ Section Review, *SE* p. 46

_____ Checking for Understanding, *TWE* p. 46

_____ Reteaching, *TWE* p. 46

_____ *Study Guide*, pp. 13–14, *TCR*

_____ *Reteaching*, p. 4, *TCR*

_____ *Supplemental Problems*, *TCR*

### Enrichment/Application

_____ Extension, *TWE* p. 46

### Close

_____ Activity, *TWE* p. 46

### Chapter Assessment

_____ Assessment, *TWE* p. 45

_____ *Alternate Assessment in the Science Classroom*

_____ *Performance Assessment in the Science Classroom*

### Multimedia Options

_____ **CD-ROM:** *Interactive Physics*

_____ **Videotape:** *MindJogger Videoquizzes*

_____ **Software:** *Computer Test Bank*

# 3.2 Lesson Plans

●●●●●●●●●●●

## Where and When?

### Section Objectives

_____ **Choose** coordinate systems for motion problems.

_____ **Differentiate** between scalar and vector quantities.

_____ **Define** a displacement vector and **determine** a time interval.

_____ **Recognize** how the chosen coordinate system affects the signs of vector quantities.

**National Science Content Standards** UCP.1, UCP.2, UCP.3; A.1, A.2, B.4, E.1

**Schedule**

Block schedule: 1/2 session

Single-period schedule: 1 session

### Focus

_____ Convergent Question, TWE p. 47

### Teach

_____ Pocket Lab, SE p. 50

_____ How It Works, SE p. 52

_____ Quick Demo, TWE p. 48

_____ Demonstration 3-1, TWE pp. 48–49

_____ Physics Journal, TWE p. 49

_____ Connections to History, TWE p. 50

_____ Physics Lab and Pocket Lab Worksheets, p. 11, TCR

_____ Physics Skills, Skill 14, TCR

_____ Spanish Resources, TCR

### Assess/Reteach

_____ Section Review, SE p. 51

_____ Checking for Understanding, TWE p. 50

_____ Reteaching, TWE p. 51

_____ Study Guide, p. 15, TCR

_____ Supplemental Problems, TCR

### Enrichment/Application

_____ Extension, TWE p. 51

_____ Critical Thinking, p. 4, TCR

### Close

_____ Activity, TWE p. 51

### Chapter Assessment

_____ Assessment, TWE p. 49

_____ Alternate Assessment in the Science Classroom

_____ Performance Assessment in the Science Classroom

### Multimedia Options

_____ **CD-ROM:** What Is Physics?; Mathematical Relationships; Vectors; Velocity, PCA

_____ **Videotape:** MindJogger Videoquizzes

_____ **Videodisc:** STVS Earth and Space, Disc 3, Side 1, Ch. 15

_____ **Software:** Computer Test Bank

Date _____ Period _____ Name _____

# 3.3 Lesson Plans

## Velocity and Acceleration

### Section Objectives

_____ **Define** *velocity* and *acceleration* operationally.
_____ **Relate** the direction and magnitude of velocity and acceleration vectors to the motion of objects.
_____ **Create** pictorial and physical models for solving motion problems.

**National Science Content Standards** UCP.1, UCP.2, UCP.3; A.1, B.4, D.1, F.6, G.2
**Schedule**
Block schedule: 2 sessions
Single-period schedule: 3 sessions

### Focus

_____ Activity, *TWE* p. 53

### Teach

_____ Pocket Lab, *SE* p. 55
_____ Earth Science Connection, *SE* p. 56
_____ Design Your Own Physics Lab, *SE* p. 58
_____ Quick Demo, *TWE* p. 53
_____ Tech Prep, *TWE* p. 53

_____ Physics Journal, *TWE* p. 54
_____ Demonstration 3-2, *TWE* pp. 54–55
_____ Applying Physics, *TWE* p. 57
_____ *Physics Lab and Pocket Lab Worksheets, pp. 9–10, 12, TCR*

### Assess/Reteach

_____ Section Review, *SE* p. 59
_____ Checking for Understanding, *TWE* p. 59
_____ Reteaching, *TWE* p. 59

_____ *Study Guide, p. 16, TCR*
_____ *Supplemental Problems, TCR*

### Enrichment/Application

_____ Extension, *TWE* p. 59
_____ Cultural Diversity, *TWE* p. 56

_____ *Enrichment, pp. 5–6, TCR*

### Close

_____ Activity, *TWE* p. 59

### Chapter Assessment

_____ Chapter Review, *SE* pp. 60–61
_____ Assessment, *TWE* p. 57
_____ Chapter Assessment, pp. 9–12, *TCR*

_____ *Alternate Assessment in the Science Classroom*
_____ *Performance Assessment in the Science Classroom*

### Multimedia Options

_____ **CD-ROM:** Vectors; Acceleration, *PCA*
_____ **Videotape:** *MindJogger Videoquizzes*

_____ **Videodisc:** *STVS Physics, Disc 1, Side 2, Ch. 7*
_____ **Software:** *Computer Test Bank*

# 4.1 Lesson Plans

**KEY**
*SE* = Student Edition, *TWE* = Teacher Wraparound Edition, *TCR* = Teacher Classroom Resources, *STVS* = Science and Technology Videodisc Series, *PCA* = Physics for the Computer Age

## Properties of Vectors

### Section Objectives

_____ **Determine** graphically the sum of the magnitudes of two or more vectors.
_____ **Solve** problems of relative velocity.

**National Science Content Standards** UCP.1, UCP.2, UCP.3, UCP.4; A.1, B.4, C.6, E.1, F.1, G.1
**Schedule**
Block schedule: 1 1/2 sessions
Single-period schedule: 2 sessions

### Focus

_____ Activity, *TWE* p. 64

### Teach

_____ Fine Arts Connection, *SE* p. 64
_____ Using a Calculator, *SE* p. 67
_____ Help Wanted, *SE* p. 68
_____ Physics Lab, *SE* p. 69
_____ Physics & Society, *SE* p. 70
_____ Tech Prep, *TWE* p. 65
_____ Demonstration 4-1, *TWE* pp. 66–67
_____ Physics Journal, *TWE* p. 68

_____ Applying Physics, *TWE* p. 68
_____ Transparency 4 Master and Worksheet, pp. 9–10, *TCR*
_____ *Physics Lab and Pocket Lab Worksheets, pp. 13–15, TCR*
_____ *Laboratory Manual,* Lab 4.1, *TCR*
_____ *Spanish Resources, TCR*

### Assess/Reteach

_____ Section Review, *SE* p. 71
_____ Checking for Understanding, *TWE* p. 71
_____ Reteaching, *TWE* p. 71

_____ *Study Guide,* pp. 17–22, *TCR*
_____ *Supplemental Problems, TCR*

### Enrichment/Application

_____ Extension, *TWE* p. 71

_____ *Enrichment,* pp. 7–8, *TCR*

### Close

_____ Closing Strategy, *TWE* p. 71

### Chapter Assessment

_____ Assessment, *TWE* p. 65
_____ *Alternate Assessment in the Science Classroom*

_____ *Performance Assessment in the Science Classroom*

### Multimedia Options

_____ **CD-ROM:** *Interactive Physics*
_____ **CD-ROM:** Velocity; Mathematical Relationships, *PCA*

_____ **Videotape:** *MindJogger Videoquizzes*
_____ **Software:** *Computer Test Bank*

# 4.2 Lesson Plans

**KEY**
*SE* = Student Edition, *TWE* = Teacher Wraparound Edition, *TCR* = Teacher Classroom Resources, *STVS* = Science and Technology Videodisc Series, *PCA* = Physics for the Computer Age

## Components of Vectors

### Section Objectives

_____ **Establish** a coordinate system in problems involving vector quantities.

_____ **Use** the process of resolution of vectors to find the components of vectors.

_____ **Determine** algebraically the sum of two or more vectors by adding the components of the vectors.

**National Science Content Standards** UCP.1, UCP.2, UCP.3, UCP.4; A.1, B.4, E.1, G.1, G.3

**Schedule**

Block schedule: 2 1/2 sessions

Single-period schedule: 4 sessions

### Focus

_____ Focus Strategy, *TWE* p. 72

### Teach

_____ Pocket Lab, *SE* p. 74

_____ Quick Demo, *TWE* p. 73

_____ Connections to Mathematics, *TWE* p. 73

_____ Physics Journal, *TWE* p. 74

_____ Demonstration 4-2, *TWE* pp. 74–75

_____ Transparency 5 Master and Worksheet, pp. 11–12, *TCR*

_____ *Physics Lab and Pocket Lab Worksheets, p. 16, TCR*

_____ *Spanish Resources, TCR*

### Assess/Reteach

_____ Section Review, *SE* p. 76

_____ Checking for Understanding, *TWE* p. 76

_____ Reteaching, *TWE* p. 76

_____ Study Guide, pp. 23–24, *TCR*

_____ Reteaching, p. 5, *TCR*

_____ *Supplemental Problems, TCR*

### Enrichment/Application

_____ Extension, *TWE* p. 76

_____ *Critical Thinking, pp. 6–7, TCR*

### Close

_____ Convergent Question, *TWE* p. 76

### Chapter Assessment

_____ Chapter Review, *SE* pp. 77–79

_____ Assessment, *TWE* p. 72

_____ *Chapter Assessment, pp. 13–16, TCR*

_____ *Alternate Assessment in the Science Classroom*

_____ *Performance Assessment in the Science Classroom*

### Multimedia Options

_____ **CD-ROM:** Acceleration; Vectors, *PCA*

_____ **Videotape:** *MindJogger Videoquizzes*

_____ **Software:** *Computer Test Bank*

# 5.1 Lesson Plans

**KEY**
*SE* = Student Edition, *TWE* = Teacher Wraparound Edition, *TCR* = Teacher Classroom Resources, *STVS* = Science and Technology Videodisc Series, *PCA* = Physics for the Computer Age

## Graphing Motion in One Dimension

### Section Objectives

_____ **Interpret** graphs of position versus time for a moving object to determine the velocity of the object.

_____ **Describe** in words the information presented in graphs and **draw** graphs from descriptions of motion.

_____ **Write** equations that describe the position of an object moving at constant velocity.

**National Science Content Standards** UCP.1, UCP.2, UCP.3; A.1, A.2, B.4, G.2

**Schedule**
Block schedule: 1 session
Single-period schedule: 1 session

### Focus

_____ Focus Strategy, *TWE* p. 82

### Teach

_____ Pocket Lab, *SE* p. 87

_____ Earth Science Connection, *SE* p. 89

_____ Quick Demos, *TWE* pp. 81, 84

_____ Tech Prep, *TWE* p. 84

_____ Physics Journal, *TWE* p. 85

_____ Demonstration 5-1, *TWE* pp. 86-87

_____ Connections to Biology, *TWE* p. 88

_____ Transparencies 6, 7 Masters and Worksheets, pp. 13–16, *TCR*

_____ *Physics Lab and Pocket Lab Worksheets*, p. 19, *TCR*

_____ *Spanish Resources, TCR*

### Assess/Reteach

_____ Section Review, *SE* p. 89

_____ Checking for Understanding, *TWE* p. 89

_____ Reteaching, *TWE* p. 89

_____ *Study Guide*, pp. 25–27, *TCR*

_____ *Supplemental Problems, TCR*

### Enrichment/Application

_____ Cultural Diversity, *TWE* p. 83

_____ Enrichment, *TWE* p. 88

_____ Extension, *TWE* p. 89

_____ *Enrichment*, pp. 9–10, *TCR*

### Close

_____ Closing Strategy, *TWE* p. 89

### Chapter Assessment

_____ Assessment, *TWE* p. 84

_____ *Alternate Assessment in the Science Classroom*

_____ *Performance Assessment in the Science Classroom*

### Multimedia Options

_____ CD-ROM: *Interactive Physics*

_____ Videotape: *MindJogger Videoquizzes*

_____ **Software:** *Computer Test Bank*

# 5.2 Lesson Plans
•••••••••••

**KEY**
*SE* = Student Edition, *TWE* = Teacher Wraparound Edition, *TCR* = Teacher Classroom Resources, *STVS* = Science and Technology Videodisc Series, *PCA* = Physics for the Computer Age

## Graphing Velocity in One Dimension

### Section Objectives

_____ **Determine**, from a graph of velocity versus time, the velocity of an object at a specified time.

_____ **Interpret** a *v-t* graph to find the time at which an object has a specific velocity.

_____ **Calculate** the displacement of an object from the area under a *v-t* curve.

**National Science Content Standards** UCP.1, UCP.2, UCP.3; A.1, A.2, B.4, G.2

**Schedule**
Block schedule: 1 1/2 sessions
Single-period schedule: 2 sessions

### Focus
_____ Focus Strategy, *TWE* p. 90

### Teach
_____ Pocket Labs, *SE* pp. 91, 93
_____ Quick Demo, *TWE* p. 90
_____ Physics Journal, *TWE* p. 92
_____ Demonstration 5-2, *TWE* pp. 90–91

_____ Physics Lab and Pocket Lab Worksheets, pp. 20–21, *TCR*
_____ Spanish Resources, *TCR*

### Assess/Reteach
_____ Section Review, *SE* p. 93
_____ Checking for Understanding, *TWE* p. 92
_____ Reteaching, *TWE* p. 92

_____ Study Guide, p. 28, *TCR*
_____ Reteaching, p. 6, *TCR*
_____ Supplemental Problems, *TCR*

### Enrichment/Application
_____ Extension, *TWE* p. 93

_____ Advanced Concepts in Physics, pp. 51–60, *TCR*

### Close
_____ Closing Strategy, *TWE* p. 93

### Chapter Assessment
_____ Assessment, *TWE* p. 92
_____ Alternate Assessment in the Science Classroom

_____ Performance Assessment in the Science Classroom

### Multimedia Options
_____ **Videotape:** *MindJogger Videoquizzes*

_____ **Software:** *Computer Test Bank*

# 5.3 Lesson Plans

**KEY**
*SE* = Student Edition, *TWE* = Teacher Wraparound Edition, *TCR* = Teacher Classroom Resources, *STVS* = Science and Technology Videodisc Series, *PCA* = Physics for the Computer Age

## Acceleration

### Section Objectives

_____ **Determine** from the curves on a velocity-time graph both the constant and instantaneous acceleration.

_____ **Determine** the sign of acceleration using a *v-t* graph and a motion diagram.

_____ **Calculate** the velocity and the displacement of an object undergoing constant acceleration.

**National Science Content Standards** UCP.1, UCP.2, UCP.3, UCP.4; A.1, A.2, B.4, E.1, E.2, G.1

**Schedule**
Block schedule: 1 session
Single-period schedule: 2 sessions

### Focus

_____ Focus Strategy, *TWE* p. 94

### Teach

_____ Physics & Technology, *SE* p. 95
_____ Help Wanted, *SE* p. 98
_____ Pocket Lab, *SE* p. 99
_____ Design Your Own Physics Lab, *SE* p. 100
_____ Connections to Mathematics, *TWE* p. 95
_____ Tech Prep, *TWE* p. 95
_____ Demonstration 5-3, *TWE* pp. 96–97
_____ Physics Journal, *TWE* p. 98

_____ Quick Demo, *TWE* p. 101
_____ Applying Physics, *TWE* p. 102
_____ *Graphing Calculators in the Science Classroom*
_____ *Laboratory Manual*, Lab 5.1, *TCR*
_____ *Physics Lab and Pocket Lab Worksheets*, pp. 17–18, 22, *TCR*
_____ *Spanish Resources, TCR*

### Assess/Reteach

_____ Section Review, *SE* p. 103
_____ Checking for Understanding, *TWE* p. 103
_____ Reteaching, *TWE* p. 103

_____ *Study Guide*, p. 29, *TCR*
_____ *Supplemental Problems, TCR*

### Enrichment/Application

_____ Extension, *TWE* p. 103

_____ *Critical Thinking*, p. 8, *TCR*

### Close

_____ Closing Strategy, *TWE* p. 103

### Chapter Assessment

_____ Assessment, *TWE* p. 97
_____ *Alternate Assessment in the Science Classroom*

_____ *Performance Assessment in the Science Classroom*

### Multimedia Options

_____ **Videotape:** *MindJogger Videoquizzes*
_____ **Videotape:** *The Mechanical Universe*, Quad 3

_____ **Videodisc:** *STVS* Physics, Disc 1, Side 1, Ch. 4
_____ **Software:** *Computer Test Bank*

# 5.4 Lesson Plans

## Free Fall

### Section Objectives

_____ **Recognize** the meaning of the acceleration due to gravity.

_____ **Define** the magnitude of the acceleration due to gravity as a positive quantity and **determine** the sign of the acceleration relative to the chosen coordinate system.

_____ **Use** the motion equations to solve problems involving freely falling objects.

**National Science Content Standards** UCP.1, UCP.2, UCP.3, UCP.4; A.1, A.2, B.4, D.1, E.1, E.2, G.1, G.2, G.3

**Schedule**

Block schedule: 1 1/2 sessions

Single-period schedule: 3 sessions

### Focus

_____ Focus Strategy, *TWE* p. 104

### Teach

_____ Quick Demo, *TWE* p. 105

_____ Physics Journal, *TWE* p. 106

_____ *Laboratory Manual*, Lab 5.2, *TCR*

_____ *Physics Skills*, Skill 15 p. 33, *TCR*

_____ *Spanish Resources*, *TCR*

### Assess/Reteach

_____ Section Review, *SE* p.106

_____ Checking for Understanding, *TWE* p. 106

_____ Reteaching, *TWE* p. 106

_____ *Study Guide*, p. 30, *TCR*

_____ *Supplemental Problems*, *TCR*

### Enrichment/Application

_____ Extension, *TWE* p. 106

### Close

_____ Closing Strategy, *TWE* p. 106

### Chapter Assessment

_____ Chapter Review, *SE* pp. 107–115

_____ Assessment, *TWE* p. 105

_____ *Chapter Assessment*, pp. 17–22, *TCR*

_____ *Alternate Assessment in the Science Classroom*

_____ *Performance Assessment in the Science Classroom*

### Multimedia Options

_____ **CD-ROM:** Mathematical Relationships; Acceleration, *PCA*

_____ **Videotape:** *MindJogger Videoquizzes*

_____ **Software:** *Computer Test Bank*

# 6.1 Lesson Plans

......**........

## Force and Motion

### Section Objectives

_____ **Define** a force and **differentiate** between contact forces and long-range forces.

_____ **Recognize** the significance of Newton's second law of motion and use it to solve motion problems.

_____ **Explain** the meaning of Newton's first law and **describe** an object in equilibrium.

**National Science Content Standards** UCP.1, UCP.2, UCP.3, UCP.4; A.1, A.2, B.4, B.6, D.1, G.1, G.2, G.3

**Schedule**
Block schedule: 1 session
Single-period schedule: 2 sessions

### Focus

_____ Discrepant Event, *TWE* p. 118

### Teach

_____ Pocket Labs, *SE* pp. 119, 123

_____ Help Wanted, *SE* p. 122

_____ Quick Demos, *TWE* pp. 117, 122

_____ Connections to Rocketry, *TWE* p. 121

_____ Demonstration 6-1, *TWE* pp. 122–123

_____ Physics Journal, *TWE* p. 123

_____ *Physics Lab and Pocket Lab Worksheets, pp. 26–27, TCR*

_____ *Laboratory Manual, Lab 6.1, TCR*

_____ *Spanish Resources, TCR*

### Assess/Reteach

_____ Section Review, *SE* p. 125

_____ Checking for Understanding, *TWE* p. 125

_____ Reteaching, *TWE* p. 125

_____ *Study Guide, pp. 31–33, TCR*

_____ *Reteaching, pp. 7–8, TCR*

_____ *Supplemental Problems, TCR*

### Enrichment/Application

_____ Cultural Diversity, *TWE* p. 119

_____ Extension, *TWE* p. 125

_____ *Enrichment, pp. 11–12, TCR*

_____ *Tech Prep Applications, pp. 5–8, TCR*

_____ *Advanced Concepts in Physics, pp. 9–14, TCR*

### Close

_____ Closing Strategy, *TWE* p. 125

### Chapter Assessment

_____ Assessment, *TWE* p. 121

_____ *Alternate Assessment in the Science Classroom*

_____ *Performance Assessment in the Science Classroom*

### Multimedia Options

_____ **CD-ROM:** *Interactive Physics*

_____ **CD-ROM:** Mathematical Relationships; Forces, *PCA*

_____ **Videotape:** *MindJogger Videoquizzes*

_____ **Videotape:** *The Mechanical Universe,* Quads 1, 3

_____ **Videodisc:** *STVS Physics,* Disc 1, Side 1, Ch. 2

_____ **Software:** *Computer Test Bank*

# 6.2 Lesson Plans

KEY
*SE* = Student Edition, *TWE* = Teacher Wraparound Edition, *TCR* = Teacher Classroom Resources, *STVS* = Science and Technology Videodisc Series, *PCA* = Physics for the Computer Age

## Using Newton's Laws

### Section Objectives

_____ **Describe** how the weight and the mass of an object are related.

_____ **Differentiate** between the gravitational force weight and what is experienced as apparent weight.

_____ **Define** the friction force and **distinguish** between static and kinetic friction.

_____ **Describe** simple harmonic motion and **explain** how the acceleration due to gravity influences such motion.

**National Science Content Standards** UCP.1, UCP.2, UCP.3, UCP.4, UCP.5; A.1, A.2, B.4, B.6, D.1, E.1, G.1, G.2, G.3

**Schedule**

Block schedule: 2 sessions

Single-period schedule: 3 sessions

### Focus

_____ Focus Strategy, *TWE* p. 127

### Teach

_____ Pocket Labs, *SE* pp. 129, 133

_____ Earth Science Connection, *SE* p. 130

_____ Physics Lab, *SE* p. 137

_____ Quick Demos, *TWE* pp. 127, 130

_____ Physics Journal, *TWE* pp. 129, 130

_____ Applying Physics, *TWE* p. 131

_____ Demonstration 6–2, *TWE* pp. 132–133

_____ Tech Prep, *TWE* p. 134

_____ *Physics Lab and Pocket Lab Worksheets, pp. 23–25, 28–29, TCR*

_____ *Laboratory Manual,* Lab 6.2, *TCR*

_____ *Physics Skills,* Skill 15 p. 34, *TCR*

_____ *Spanish Resources, TCR*

### Assess/Reteach

_____ Section Review, *SE* p. 136

_____ Checking for Understanding, *TWE* p. 135

_____ Reteaching, *TWE* p. *135*

_____ *Study Guide,* pp. 34–35, *TCR*

_____ *Supplemental Problems, TCR*

### Enrichment/Application

_____ Enrichment, *TWE* pp. 130, 132, 135

_____ Extension, *TWE* p. 136

_____ *Advanced Concepts in Physics,* pp. 1–14, *TCR*

### Close

_____ Closing Strategy, *TWE* p. 136

### Chapter Assessment

_____ Assessment, *TWE* p. 134

_____ *Alternate Assessment in the Science Classroom*

_____ *Performance Assessment in the Science Classroom*

### Multimedia Options

_____ **Videotape:** *MindJogger Videoquizzes*

_____ **Videotape:** *The Mechanical Universe,* Quad 1

_____ **Videodisc:** *STVS* Physics, Disc 1, Side 1, Chs. 3,4; Disc 1, Side 2, Ch. 2

_____ **Software:** *Computer Test Bank*

# 6.3 Lesson Plans

**KEY**
*SE* = Student Edition, *TWE* = Teacher Wraparound Edition, *TCR* = Teacher Classroom Resources, *STVS* = Science and Technology Videodisc Series, *PCA* = Physics for the Computer Age

## Interaction Forces

### Section Objectives

_____ **Explain** the meaning of interaction pairs of forces and how they are related by Newton's third law.

_____ **List** the four fundamental forces and **illustrate** the environment in which each can be observed.

_____ **Explain** the tension in ropes and strings in terms of Newton's third law.

**National Science Content Standards** UCP.1, UCP.2, UCP.3, UCP.4; A.1, B.4, B.6, G.1, G.2, G.3

**Schedule**

Block schedule: 1 1/2 sessions

Single-period schedule: 3 sessions

### Focus

_____ Focus Strategy, *TWE* p. 138

### Teach

_____ Pocket Lab, *SE* p. 141

_____ How It Works, *SE* p. 142

_____ Quick Demo, *TWE* p. 139

_____ Physics Journal, *TWE* p. 140

_____ Transparency 8 Master and Worksheet, pp. 17–18, *TCR*

_____ *Physics Lab and Pocket Lab Worksheets, p. 30, TCR*

_____ *Laboratory Manual, Lab 6.3, TCR*

_____ *Spanish Resources, TCR*

### Assess/Reteach

_____ Section Review, *SE* p. 143

_____ Checking for Understanding, *TWE* p. 143

_____ Reteaching, *TWE* p. 143

_____ *Study Guide, p. 36, TCR*

_____ *Supplemental Problems, TCR*

### Enrichment/Application

_____ Extension, *TWE* p. 143

_____ *Advanced Concepts in Physics, pp. 9–14, TCR*

_____ *Critical Thinking, p. 9, TCR*

### Close

_____ Closing Strategy, *TWE* p. 143

### Chapter Assessment

_____ Chapter Review, *SE* pp. 144–147

_____ Assessment, *TWE* p. 139

_____ *Chapter Assessment, pp. 23–28, TCR*

_____ *Alternate Assessment in the Science Classroom*

_____ *Performance Assessment in the Science Classroom*

### Multimedia Options

_____ **Videotape:** *MindJogger Videoquizzes*

_____ **Videotape:** *The Mechanical Universe*, Quad 2

_____ **Videodisc:** *STVS* Physics, Disc 1, Side 2, Chs. 4, 5

_____ **Software:** *Computer Test Bank*

# 7.1 Lesson Plans

## Forces in Two Dimensions

### Section Objectives

_____ **Determine** the force that produces equilibrium when three forces act on an object.

_____ **Analyze** the motion of an object on an inclined plane with and without friction.

**National Science Content Standards** UCP.1, UCP.2, UCP.3, UCP.4; A.2, B.4

**Schedule**

Block schedule: 1 session

Single-period schedule: 2 sessions

### Focus

_____ Focus Strategy, *TWE* p. 150

### Teach

_____ Quick Demos, *TWE* pp. 149, 150

_____ Applying Physics, *TWE* p. 151

_____ Demonstration 7–1, *TWE* pp. 152–153

_____ Physics Journal, *TWE* p. 153

_____ Connections to Biology, *TWE* p. 153

_____ Transparency 9 Master and Worksheet, pp. 19–20, *TCR*

_____ *Graphing Calculators in the Science Classroom*

_____ Laboratory Manual, Labs 7.1, 7.2, *TCR*

_____ Spanish Resources, *TCR*

### Assess/Reteach

_____ Section Review, *SE* p. 154

_____ Checking for Understanding, *TWE* p. 153

_____ Reteaching, *TWE* p. 154

_____ Study Guide, pp. 37–39, *TCR*

_____ Reteaching, pp. 9–10, *TCR*

_____ Supplemental Problems, *TCR*

### Enrichment/Application

_____ Cultural Diversity, *TWE* p. 151

_____ Extension, *TWE* p. 154

_____ Tech Prep Applications, pp. 9–12, *TCR*

### Close

_____ Closing Strategy, *TWE* p. 154

### Chapter Assessment

_____ Assessment, *TWE* p. 152

_____ Alternate Assessment in the Science Classroom

_____ Performance Assessment in the Science Classroom

### Multimedia Options

_____ **CD-ROM**: *Interactive Physics*

_____ **Videotape**: *MindJogger Videoquizzes*

_____ **Software**: *Computer Test Bank*

# 7.2 Lesson Plans

**KEY**
*SE* = Student Edition, *TWE* = Teacher Wraparound Edition, *TCR* = Teacher Classroom Resources, *STVS* = Science and Technology Videodisc Series, *PCA* = Physics for the Computer Age

## Projectile Motion

### Section Objectives

_____ **Recognize** that the vertical and horizontal motions of a projectile are independent.

_____ **Relate** the height, time in the air, and initial vertical velocity of a projectile using its vertical motion, then **determine** the range.

_____ **Explain** how the shape of the trajectory of a moving object depends upon the frame of reference from which it is observed.

**National Science Content Standards** UCP.1, UCP.2, UCP.3; A.2, B.4, C.6, E.2, G.1, G.2

**Schedule**

Block schedule: 2 sessions

Single-period schedule: 3 sessions

### Focus

_____ Focus Strategy, *TWE* p. 156

### Teach

_____ Pocket Lab, *SE* p. 156

_____ Biology Connection, *SE* p. 161

_____ Design Your Own Physics Lab, *SE* p. 162

_____ Quick Demo, *TWE* p. 156

_____ Applying Physics, *TWE* p. 157

_____ Physics Journal, *TWE* p. 158

_____ Transparency 10 Master and Worksheet, pp. 21–22, *TCR*

_____ *Physics Lab and Pocket Lab Worksheets, pp. 31–34, TCR*

_____ *Laboratory Manual, Lab 7.3, TCR*

_____ *Spanish Resources, TCR*

### Assess/Reteach

_____ Section Review, *SE* p.161

_____ Checking for Understanding, *TWE* p. 161

_____ Reteaching, *TWE* p. 161

_____ *Study Guide, pp. 40–41, TCR*

_____ *Supplemental Problems, TCR*

### Enrichment/Application

_____ Extension, *TWE* p. 161

_____ *Advanced Concepts in Physics, pp. 15–30, TCR*

### Close

_____ Closing Strategy, *TWE* p. 161

### Chapter Assessment

_____ Assessment, *TWE* p. 157

_____ *Alternate Assessment in the Science Classroom*

_____ *Performance Assessment in the Science Classroom*

### Multimedia Options

_____ **CD-ROM:** 2-D Motion, *PCA*

_____ **Videotape:** *MindJogger Videoquizzes*

_____ **Software:** *Computer Test Bank*

**KEY**
*SE* = Student Edition, *TWE* = Teacher Wraparound Edition, *TCR* = Teacher Classroom Resources, *STVS* = Science and Technology Videodisc Series, *PCA* = Physics for the Computer Age

# 7.3 Lesson Plans

## Circular Motion

### Section Objectives

_____ **Explain** the acceleration of an object moving in a circle at constant speed.

_____ **Describe** how centripetal acceleration depends upon the object's speed and the radius of the circle.

_____ **Recognize** the direction of the force that causes centripetal acceleration.

_____ **Explain** how the rate of circular motion is changed by exerting torque on it.

**National Science Content Standards** UCP.1, UCP.2, UCP.3; B.4, E.1, E.2, G.2
**Schedule**
Block schedule: 1 1/2 sessions
Single-period schedule: 3 sessions

### Focus

_____ Focus Strategy, *TWE* p. 163

### Teach

_____ Pocket Labs, *SE* pp. 164, 166

_____ Help Wanted, *SE* p. 165

_____ Physics & Technology, *SE* p. 167

_____ Quick Demo, *TWE* p. 164

_____ Tech Prep, *TWE* p. 164

_____ Physics Journal, *TWE* p. 165

_____ Demonstration 7–2, *TWE* pp. 166–167

_____ *Physics Lab and Pocket Lab Worksheets, pp. 35–36, TCR*

_____ *Spanish Resources, TCR*

### Assess/Reteach

_____ Section Review, *SE* p. 168

_____ Checking for Understanding, *TWE* p. 168

_____ Reteaching, *TWE* p. 168

_____ *Study Guide, p. 42, TCR*

_____ *Supplemental Problems, TCR*

### Enrichment/Application

_____ Enrichment, *TWE* p. 165

_____ Extension, *TWE* p. 168

_____ *Critical Thinking, p. 10, TCR*

_____ *Enrichment, pp. 13–14, TCR*

### Close

_____ Closing Strategy, *TWE* p. 168

### Chapter Assessment

_____ Chapter Review, *SE* pp. 169–173

_____ Assessment, *TWE* p. 165

_____ *Chapter Assessment, pp. 29–34, TCR*

_____ *Alternate Assessment in the Science Classroom*

_____ *Performance Assessment in the Science Classroom*

### Multimedia Options

_____ **CD-ROM:** 2-D Motion; Energy, *PCA*

_____ **Videotape:** *MindJogger Videoquizzes*

_____ **Videotape:** *The Mechanical Universe*, Quad 3

_____ **Videodisc:** *STVS* Physics, Disc 1, Side 2, Ch. 8

_____ **Software:** *Computer Test Bank*

# 8.1 Lesson Plans

## Motion in the Heavens and on Earth

### Section Objectives

____ **Relate** Kepler's laws of planetary motion to Newton's law of universal gravitation.

____ **Calculate** the periods and speeds of orbiting objects.

____ **Describe** the method Cavendish used to measure *G* and the results of knowing *G*.

**National Science Content Standards** UCP.1, UCP.2, UCP.3; A.1, A.2, B.2, B.4, B.6, D.3, D.4, G.1, G.2, G.3

**Schedule**

Block schedule: 1 session

Single-period schedule: 2 sessions

### Focus

____ Discrepant Event, *TWE* p. 176

### Teach

____ Pocket Lab, *SE* p. 177

____ Physics & Technology, *SE* p. 178

____ Physics Lab, *SE* p. 179

____ Using a Calculator, *SE* p. 181

____ Demonstration 8-1, *TWE* pp. 180–181

____ Applying Physics, *TWE* p. 180

____ Physics Journal, *TWE* p. 182

____ Quick Demo, *TWE* p. 183

____ Transparencies 11, 12 Masters and Worksheets, pp. 23–26, *TCR*

____ *Graphing Calculators in the Science Classroom*

____ *Physics Lab and Pocket Lab Worksheets,* pp. 37–39, *TCR*

____ *Laboratory Manual,* Lab 8.1, *TCR*

____ *Spanish Resources, TCR*

### Assess/Reteach

____ Section Review, *SE* p. 184

____ Checking for Understanding, *TWE* p. 183

____ Reteaching, *TWE* p. 184

____ *Study Guide,* pp. 43–46, *TCR*

____ Supplemental Problems, *TCR*

### Enrichment/Application

____ Cultural Diversity, *TWE* p. 177

____ Enrichment, *TWE* p. 183

____ Extension, *TWE* p. 184

____ *Enrichment,* pp. 15–16, *TCR*

### Close

____ Closing Strategy, *TWE* p. 184

### Chapter Assessment

____ Assessment, *TWE* p. 181

____ *Alternate Assessment in the Science Classroom*

____ *Performance Assessment in the Science Classroom*

### Multimedia Options

____ CD-ROM: *Interactive Physics*

____ CD-ROM: *Velocity; Orbital Motion, PCA*

____ Videotape: *MindJogger Videoquizzes*

____ Videotape: *The Mechanical Universe,* Quads 1, 4

____ Software: *Computer Test Bank*

Date _____    Period _____    Name _____

**KEY**
*SE* = Student Edition, *TWE* = Teacher Wraparound Edition, *TCR* = Teacher Classroom Resources, *STVS* = Science and Technology Videodisc Series, *PCA* = Physics for the Computer Age

# 8.2 Lesson Plans

## Using the Law of Universal Gravitation

### Section Objectives

_____ **Solve** problems involving orbital speed and period.
_____ **Relate** weightlessness to objects in free fall.
_____ **Describe** gravitational fields.
_____ **Distinguish** between inertial mass and gravitational mass.
_____ **Contrast** Newton's and Einstein's views about gravitation.

**National Science Content Standards** UCP.1, UCP.2, UCP.3, UCP.4; A.1, A.2, B.4, B.6, D.3, D.4, G.1, G.2, G.3
**Schedule**
Block schedule: 2 1/2 sessions
Single-period schedule: 4 sessions

### Focus

_____ Quick Demo, *TWE* p. 185

### Teach

_____ Help Wanted, *SE* p. 186
_____ Pocket Labs, *SE* pp. 188, 189
_____ Literature Connection, *SE* p. 190
_____ Quick Demos, *TWE* pp. 186, 190
_____ Physics Journal, *TWE* p. 188
_____ Connections to Biology, *TWE* p. 188
_____ Tech Prep, *TWE* p. 189

_____ Demonstration 8-2, *TWE* pp. 190–191
_____ Transparency 12 Master and Worksheet, pp. 25–26, *TCR*
_____ *Physics Lab and Pocket Lab Worksheets, pp. 40–41, TCR*
_____ *Spanish Resources, TCR*

### Assess/Reteach

_____ Section Review, *SE* p. 192
_____ Checking for Understanding, *TWE* p. 191
_____ Reteaching, *TWE* p. 192

_____ *Study Guide, pp. 47–48, TCR*
_____ *Reteaching, p. 11, TCR*
_____ *Supplemental Problems, TCR*

### Enrichment/Application

_____ Extension, *TWE* p. 192

_____ *Critical Thinking, pp. 11–12, TCR*

### Close

_____ Quick Demo, *TWE* p. 192

### Chapter Assessment

_____ Chapter Review, *SE* pp. 193–197
_____ Assessment, *TWE* p. 186
_____ *Chapter Assessment, pp. 35–38, TCR*

_____ *Alternate Assessment in the Science Classroom*
_____ *Performance Assessment in the Science Classroom*

### Multimedia Options

_____ **Videotape:** *MindJogger Videoquizzes*
_____ **Videotape:** *The Mechanical Universe,* Quads 1, 4

_____ **Videodisc:** *STVS* Earth and Space, Disc 3, Side 1, Chs. 2, 6, 11, 12
_____ **Software:** *Computer Test Bank*

# 9.1 Lesson Plans

## Impulse and Momentum

### Section Objectives

_____ **Compare** the system before and after an event
in momentum problems.

_____ **Define** the momentum of an object.

_____ **Determine** the impulse given to an object.

_____ **Recognize** that impulse equals the change in
momentum of an object.

**National Science Content Standards** UCP.1,
UCP.2, UCP.3, UCP.5; A.2, B.4, B.6, D.1, E.1, F.1

**Schedule**

Block schedule: 1 session

Single-period schedule: 1 session

### Focus

_____ Uncovering Misconceptions, *TWE* p. 200

### Teach

_____ Physics & Technology, *SE* p. 202

_____ Pocket Lab, *SE* p. 205

_____ Fine Arts Connection, *SE* p. 205

_____ Quick Demos, *TWE* pp. 199, 201

_____ Physics Journal, *TWE* pp. 201, 203

_____ Tech Prep, *TWE* p. 202

_____ Applying Physics, *TWE* p. 203

_____ Demonstration 9-1, *TWE* pp. 204–205

_____ *Laboratory Manual*, Lab 9.2, *TCR*

_____ *Physics Lab and Pocket Lab Worksheets*,
p. 45, *TCR*

_____ Spanish Resources, *TCR*

### Assess/Reteach

_____ Section Review, *SE* p. 206

_____ Checking for Understanding, *TWE* p. 206

_____ Reteaching, *TWE* p. 206

_____ *Study Guide*, pp. 49–52, *TCR*

_____ *Supplemental Problems, TCR*

### Enrichment/Application

_____ Enrichment, *TWE* p. 204

_____ Extension, *TWE* p. 206

### Close

_____ Closing Strategy, *TWE* p. 206

### Chapter Assessment

_____ Assessment, *TWE* p. 201

_____ *Alternate Assessment in the Science Classroom*

_____ *Performance Assessment in the Science Classroom*

### Multimedia Options

_____ CD-ROM: *Interactive Physics*

_____ Videotape: *MindJogger Videoquizzes*

_____ Software: *Computer Test Bank*

# 9.2 Lesson Plans

**KEY**
*SE* = Student Edition, *TWE* = Teacher Wraparound Edition, *TCR* = Teacher Classroom Resources, *STVS* = Science and Technology Videodisc Series, *PCA* = Physics for the Computer Age

## The Conservation of Momentum

### Section Objectives

_____ **Relate** Newton's third law of motion to conservation of momentum in collisions and explosions.

_____ **Recognize** the conditions under which the momentum of a system is conserved.

_____ **Apply** conservation of momentum to explain the propulsion of rockets.

_____ **Solve** conservation of momentum problems in two dimensions by using vector analysis.

**National Science Content Standards** UCP.1, UCP.2, UCP.3; A.2, B.4, B.6

**Schedule**

Block schedule: 2 1/2 sessions

Single-period schedule: 5 sessions

### Focus

_____ Quick Demo, *TWE* p. 207

### Teach

_____ Pocket Lab, *SE* p. 208

_____ Using a Calculator, *SE* p. 210

_____ Physics Lab, *SE* p. 213

_____ Help Wanted, *SE* p. 214

_____ Quick Demo, *TWE* p. 208

_____ Demonstration 9-2, *TWE* pp. 208–209

_____ Connections to Biology, *TWE* p. 214

_____ Physics Journal, *TWE* p. 215

_____ Transparency 13 Master and Worksheet, pp. 27–28, *TCR*

_____ *Laboratory Manual*, Lab 9.1, *TCR*

_____ *Physics Lab and Pocket Lab Worksheets*, pp. 43–44, 46, *TCR*

_____ *Spanish Resources*, *TCR*

### Assess/Reteach

_____ Section Review, *SE* p. 216

_____ Checking for Understanding, *TWE* p. 216

_____ Reteaching, *TWE* p. 216

_____ *Study Guide*, pp. 53–54, *TCR*

_____ *Reteaching*, pp. 12–13, *TCR*

_____ *Supplemental Problems*, *TCR*

### Enrichment/Application

_____ Cultural Diversity, *TWE* p. 211

_____ Extension, *TWE* p. 216

_____ *Enrichment*, pp. 17–18, *TCR*

_____ *Critical Thinking*, pp. 13–14, *TCR*

_____ *Tech Prep Applications*, pp. 13–16, *TCR*

### Close

_____ Closing Strategy, *TWE* p. 216

### Chapter Assessment

_____ Chapter Review, *SE* pp. 217–221

_____ Assessment, *TWE* p. 212

_____ *Chapter Assessment*, 39–44, *TCR*

_____ *Alternate Assessment in the Science Classroom*

_____ *Performance Assessment in the Science Classroom*

### Multimedia Options

_____ **CD-ROM:** Momentum, *PCA*

_____ **Videotape:** *MindJogger Videoquizzes*

_____ **Videotape:** *The Mechanical Universe*, Quad 2

_____ **Software:** *Computer Test Bank*

# 10.1 Lesson Plans

## Energy and Work

### Section Objectives

_____ **Describe** the relationship between work and energy.

_____ **Display** an ability to calculate work done by a force.

_____ **Identify** the force that does work.

_____ **Differentiate** between work and power and correctly **calculate** power used.

**National Science Content Standards** UCP.1, UCP.2, UCP.3, UCP.4; A.2, B.4, B.6

**Schedule**

Block schedule: 1 session

Single-period schedule: 2 sessions

### Focus

_____ Discrepant Event, *TWE* p. 225

### Teach

_____ Pocket Labs, *SE* pp. 225, 227

_____ Design Your Own Physics Lab, *SE* p. 232

_____ Quick Demos, *TWE* pp. 223, 228

_____ Demonstration 10-1, *TWE* pp. 226–227

_____ Demonstration 10-2, *TWE* pp. 228–229

_____ Physics Journal, *TWE* p. 229

_____ Tech Prep, *TWE* p. 230

_____ *Physics Lab and Pocket Lab Worksheets, pp. 47–50, TCR*

_____ *Spanish Resources, TCR*

### Assess/Reteach

_____ Section Review, *SE* p. 231

_____ Checking for Understanding, *TWE* p. 230

_____ Reteaching, *TWE* p. 231

_____ *Study Guide, pp. 55–57, TCR*

_____ *Supplemental Problems, TCR*

### Enrichment/Application

_____ Extension, *TWE* p. 231

### Close

_____ Closing Strategy, *TWE* p. 231

### Chapter Assessment

_____ Assessment, *TWE* pp. 226, 230

_____ *Alternate Assessment in the Science Classroom*

_____ *Performance Assessment in the Science Classroom*

### Multimedia Options

_____ CD-ROM: *Interactive Physics*

_____ Videotape: *MindJogger Videoquizzes*

_____ Software: *Computer Test Bank*

# 10.2 Lesson Plans

## Machines

### Section Objectives

_____ **Demonstrate** knowledge of why simple machines are useful.

_____ **Communicate** an understanding of mechanical advantage in ideal and real machines.

_____ **Analyze** compound machines and **describe** them in terms of simple machines.

_____ **Calculate** efficiencies for simple and compound machines.

**National Science Content Standards** UCP.1, UCP.2, UCP.3, UCP.5; B.4, B.5, B.6, C.5, E.1, E.2

**Schedule**

Block schedule: 2 sessions
Single-period schedule: 3 sessions

### Focus

_____ Discrepant Event, *TWE* p. 234

### Teach

_____ Help Wanted, *SE* p. 234

_____ Pocket Lab, *SE* p. 236

_____ How It Works, *SE* p. 240

_____ Quick Demo, *TWE* p. 234

_____ Connections to Architecture, *TWE* p. 234

_____ Applying Physics, *TWE* p. 235

_____ Physics Journal, *TWE* p. 235

_____ Connections to Biology, *TWE* p. 237

_____ Transparency 14 Master and Worksheet, pp. 29–30, *TCR*

_____ Laboratory Manual, Lab 10.1, *TCR*

_____ Physics Lab and Pocket Lab Worksheets, p. 51, *TCR*

_____ Spanish Resources, *TCR*

### Assess/Reteach

_____ Section Review, *SE* p. 239

_____ Checking for Understanding, *TWE* p. 238

_____ Reteaching, *TWE* p. 239

_____ Study Guide, pp. 58–60, *TCR*

_____ Reteaching, p. 14, *TCR*

_____ Supplemental Problems, *TCR*

### Enrichment/Application

_____ Cultural Diversity, *TWE* p. 235

_____ Enrichment, *TWE* p. 237

_____ Extension, *TWE* p. 239

_____ Tech Prep Applications, pp. 17–18, *TCR*

_____ Critical Thinking, p. 15, *TCR*

_____ Enrichment, pp. 19–20, *TCR*

### Close

_____ Quick Demo, *TWE* p. 239

### Chapter Assessment

_____ Chapter Review, *SE* pp. 241–245

_____ Assessment, *TWE* p. 238

_____ Chapter Assessment, pp. 45–48, *TCR*

_____ Alternate Assessment in the Science Classroom

_____ Performance Assessment in the Science Classroom

### Multimedia Options

_____ **Videotape:** *MindJogger Videoquizzes*

_____ **Videotape:** *The Mechanical Universe*, Quad 2

_____ **Videodisc:** *STVS* Physics, Disc 1, Side 2, Chs. 4, 9, 12, 14, 18; Chemistry, Disc 2, Side 2, Ch. 19

_____ **Software:** *Computer Test Bank*

# 11.1 Lesson Plans

**KEY**
*SE* = Student Edition, *TWE* = Teacher Wraparound Edition, *TCR* = Teacher Classroom Resources, *STVS* = Science and Technology Videodisc Series, *PCA* = Physics for the Computer Age

## The Many Forms of Energy

### Section Objectives

_____ **Use a model** to relate work and energy.
_____ **Calculate** the kinetic energy of a moving object.
_____ **Determine** how to find the gravitational potential energy of a system.
_____ **Identify** ways in which elastic potential energy is stored in a system.

**National Science Content Standards** UCP.1, UCP.2, UCP.3, UCP.4; A.1, A.2, B.4, B.6, G.1, G.2

**Schedule**
Block schedule: 1 session
Single-period schedule: 2 sessions

### Focus

_____ Focus Activity, *TWE* p. 248

### Teach

_____ Pocket Lab, *SE* p. 249
_____ Help Wanted, *SE* p. 255
_____ Design Your Own Physics Lab, *SE* p. 257
_____ Quick Demos, *TWE* pp. 247, 250, 251, 255
_____ Demonstration 11-1, *TWE* pp. 252–253
_____ *Physics Journal, TWE* p. 253

_____ Transparency 15 Master and Worksheet, pp. 31–32, *TCR*
_____ *Physics Lab and Pocket Lab Worksheets, pp. 53–55, TCR*
_____ *Physics Skills, Skill 17, TCR*
_____ *Spanish Resources, TCR*

### Assess/Reteach

_____ Section Review, *SE* p. 256
_____ Checking for Understanding, *TWE* p. 255
_____ Reteaching, *TWE* p. 256

_____ *Study Guide, pp. 61–64, TCR*
_____ *Reteaching, p. 15, TCR*
_____ *Supplemental Problems, TCR*

### Enrichment/Application

_____ Cultural Diversity, *TWE* p. 249
_____ Extension, *TWE* p. 256

_____ *Critical Thinking, p. 16, TCR*

### Close

_____ Closing Strategy, *TWE* p. 256

### Chapter Assessment

_____ Assessment, *TWE* p. 252
_____ *Alternate Assessment in the Science Classroom*

_____ *Performance Assessment in the Science Classroom*

### Multimedia Options

_____ **CD-ROM:** What Is Physics?, *PCA*
_____ **Videotape:** *MindJogger Videoquizzes*

_____ **Videodisc:** *STVS* Chemistry, Disc 2, Side 1, Ch. 5
_____ **Software:** *Computer Test Bank*

# 11.2 Lesson Plans

## Conservation of Energy

### Section Objectives

_____ **Solve** problems using the law of conservation of energy.

_____ **Analyze** collisions to find the change in kinetic energy.

**National Science Content Standards** UCP.1, UCP.2, UCP.3, UCP.4; A.2, B.4, B.5, B.6, D.1, D.3

**Schedule**

Block schedule: 2 1/2 sessions

Single-period schedule: 4 sessions

### Focus

_____ Discrepant Event, *TWE* p. 258

### Teach

_____ Pocket Lab, *SE* p. 262

_____ Earth Science Connection, *SE* p. 263

_____ Physics & Society, *SE* p. 266

_____ Quick Demos, *TWE* pp. 259, 260

_____ Physics Journal, *TWE* p. 260

_____ Demonstration 11-2, *TWE* pp. 260–261

_____ Applying Physics, *TWE* p. 262

_____ Connections to Chemistry, *TWE* p. 262

_____ Tech Prep, *TWE* p. 263

_____ Transparency 15 Master and Worksheet, pp. 31–32, *TCR*

_____ *Physics Lab and Pocket Lab Worksheets, p. 56, TCR*

_____ *Laboratory Manual, Lab 11.1, TCR*

_____ *Spanish Resources, TCR*

### Assess/Reteach

_____ Section Review, *SE* p. 265

_____ Checking for Understanding, *TWE* p. 264

_____ Reteaching, *TWE* p. 265

_____ *Study Guide, pp. 65–66, TCR*

_____ *Supplemental Problems, TCR*

### Enrichment/Application

_____ Extension, *TWE* p. 265

_____ *Tech Prep Applications, pp. 19–20, TCR*

_____ *Enrichment, pp. 21–22, TCR*

### Close

_____ Closing Strategy, *TWE* p. 265

### Chapter Assessment

_____ Chapter Review, *SE* pp. 267–271

_____ Assessment, *TWE* p. 263

_____ *Chapter Assessment, pp. 49–54, TCR*

_____ *Alternate Assessment in the Science Classroom*

_____ *Performance Assessment in the Science Classroom*

### Multimedia Options

_____ **CD-ROM:** Energy, *PCA*

_____ **Videotape:** *The Mechanical Universe,* Quad 2

_____ **Videotape:** *MindJogger Videoquizzes*

_____ **Videodisc:** *STVS* Physics, Disc 1, Side 1, Ch. 11

_____ **Software:** *Computer Test Bank*

# 12.1 Lesson Plans

## Temperature and Thermal Energy

### Section Objectives

_____ **Describe** the nature of thermal energy.

_____ **Define** temperature and **distinguish** it from thermal energy.

_____ **Use** the Celsius and Kelvin temperature scales and **convert** one to another.

_____ **Define** specific heat and **calculate** heat transfer.

**National Science Content Standards** UCP.1, UCP.2, UCP.3, UCP.4, UCP.5; A.1, A.2, B.2, B.5, B.6, F.3, G.1, G.2, G.3

**Schedule**

Block schedule: 1 session

Single-period schedule: 2 sessions

### Focus

_____ Focus Strategy, *TWE* p. 274

### Teach

_____ Physics Lab, *SE* p. 281

_____ Pocket Lab, *SE* p. 284

_____ Quick Demos, *TWE* pp. 273, 276, 279

_____ Demonstration 12-1, *TWE* p. 275

_____ Demonstration 12-2, *TWE* p. 282

_____ Physics Journal, *TWE* p. 278

_____ Applying Physics, *TWE* p. 282

_____ Connections to Chemistry, *TWE* p. 283

_____ Transparencies 16, 17 Masters and Worksheets, pp. 33–36, *TCR*

_____ *Laboratory Manual*, Lab 12.1, *TCR*

_____ *Physics Lab and Pocket Lab Worksheets*, pp. 57–59, *TCR*

_____ *Spanish Resources*, *TCR*

### Assess/Reteach

_____ Section Review, *SE* p. 284

_____ Checking for Understanding, *TWE* p. 283

_____ Reteaching, *TWE* p. 283

_____ *Study Guide*, pp. 67–69, *TCR*

_____ *Reteaching*, p.16, *TCR*

_____ *Supplemental Problems*, *TCR*

### Enrichment/Application

_____ Extension, *TWE* p. 283

_____ *Enrichment*, pp. 23–24, *TCR*

### Close

_____ Activity, *TWE* p. 283

### Chapter Assessment

_____ Assessment, *TWE* pp. 277, 282

_____ *Alternate Assessment in the Science Classroom*

_____ *Performance Assessment in the Science Classroom*

### Multimedia Options

_____ **Videotape:** *MindJogger Videoquizzes*

_____ **Videodisc:** *STVS* Physics Disc 1, Side 1, Ch. 12; Chemistry Disc 2, Side 2, Chs. 8, 10, 17

_____ **Software:** *Computer Test Bank*

# 12.2 Lesson Plans

**KEY**
*SE* = Student Edition, *TWE* = Teacher Wraparound Edition, *TCR* = Teacher Classroom Resources, *STVS* = Science and Technology Videodisc Series, *PCA* = Physics for the Computer Age

## Change of State and Laws of Thermodynamics

### Section Objectives

_____ **Define** heats of fusion and vaporization.
_____ **State** the first and second laws of thermodynamics.
_____ **Define** heat engine, refrigerator, and heat pump.
_____ **Define** entropy.

**National Science Content Standards** UCP.1, UCP.2, UCP.3, UCP.4, UCP.5; B.2, B.5, B.6, E.1, E.2, F.3, G.1

**Schedule**
Block schedule: 2 1/2 sessions
Single-period schedule: 4 sessions

### Focus

_____ Discrepant Event, *TWE* p. 285

### Teach

_____ Help Wanted, *SE* p. 286
_____ Pocket Labs, *SE* pp. 287, 294
_____ Chemistry Connection, *SE* p. 289
_____ Physics & Technology, *SE* p. 292
_____ Demonstration 12-3, *TWE* pp. 286–287
_____ Quick Demos, *TWE* pp. 288, 292
_____ Tech Prep, *TWE* p. 291

_____ Physics Journal, *TWE* p. 292
_____ Transparencies 18, 19 Masters and Worksheets, pp. 37–40, *TCR*
_____ *Laboratory Manual*, Lab 12.2, *TCR*
_____ *Physics Lab and Pocket Lab Worksheets*, pp. 60–61, *TCR*
_____ *Spanish Resources*, *TCR*

### Assess/Reteach

_____ Section Review, *SE* p. 294
_____ Checking for Understanding, *TWE* p. 293
_____ Reteaching, *TWE* p. 293

_____ *Study Guide*, pp. 70–72, *TCR*
_____ *Supplemental Problems*, *TCR*

### Enrichment/Application

_____ Enrichment, *TWE* pp. 288, 291
_____ Cultural Diversity, *TWE* p. 290

_____ Extension, *TWE* p. 293
_____ *Critical Thinking*, pp. 17–18, *TCR*

### Close

_____ Activity, *TWE* p. 294

### Chapter Assessment

_____ Chapter Review, *SE* pp. 295-297
_____ Assessment, *TWE* pp. 286, 291
_____ *Chapter Assessment*, pp. 55–58, *TCR*

_____ *Alternate Assessment in the Science Classroom*
_____ *Performance Assessment in the Science Classroom*

### Multimedia Options

_____ **Videotape:** *MindJogger Videoquizzes*
_____ **Videotape:** *The Mechanical Universe*, Quad 2
_____ **Videodisc:** *STVS* Physics Disc 1, Side 1, Chs. 8, 9; Chemistry Disc 2, Side 1, Chs. 3, 8

_____ **Software:** *Computer Test Bank*

# 13.1 Lesson Plans

**KEY**
*SE* = Student Edition, *TWE* = Teacher Wraparound Edition, *TCR* = Teacher Classroom Resources, *STVS* = Science and Technology Videodisc Series, *PCA* = Physics for the Computer Age

## The Fluid States

### Section Objectives

_____ **Describe** how fluids create pressure and **relate** Pascal's principle to some everyday occurrences.

_____ **Apply** Archimedes' and Bernoulli's principles.

_____ **Explain** how forces within liquids cause surface tension and capillary action, and **relate** the kinetic model to evaporation and condensation.

**National Science Content Standards** UCP.1, UCP.2, UCP.3, UCP.4, UCP.5; A.1, A.2, B.2, B.6, C.5, E.1, E.2, G.1

**Schedule**

Block schedule: 2 sessions

Single-period schedule: 3 sessions

### Focus

_____ Discrepant Event, *TWE* p. 300

### Teach

_____ Pocket Labs, *SE* pp. 303, 311

_____ Physics Lab, *SE* p. 308

_____ Chemistry Connection, *SE* p. 312

_____ Quick Demos, *TWE* pp. 299, 301, 302, 305, 306, 309, 312, 313

_____ Physics Journal, *TWE* pp. 303, 311

_____ Demonstration 13-1, *TWE* pp. 304–305

_____ Applying Physics, *TWE* pp. 306, 311

_____ Tech Prep, *TWE* p. 306

_____ Connections to History, *TWE* p. 312

_____ Transparency 20 Master and Worksheet, pp. 41–42, *TCR*

_____ *Physics Lab and Pocket Lab Worksheets*, pp. 63–66, *TCR*

_____ *Laboratory Manual*, Lab 13.1, *TCR*

_____ *Spanish Resources*, *TCR*

### Assess/Reteach

_____ Section Review, *SE* p. 313

_____ Checking for Understanding, *TWE* p. 312

_____ Reteaching, *TWE* p. 313

_____ *Study Guide*, pp. 73–76, *TCR*

_____ *Reteaching*, pp. 17–18, *TCR*

_____ *Supplemental Problems*, *TCR*

### Enrichment/Application

_____ Enrichment, *TWE* p. 306

_____ Cultural Diversity, *TWE* p. 310

_____ Extension, *TWE* p. 313

_____ *Enrichment*, p. 25, *TCR*

### Close

_____ Closing Strategy, TWE p. 313

### Chapter Assessment

_____ Assessment, *TWE* pp. 303, 307, 311

_____ *Alternate Assessment in the Science Classroom*

_____ *Performance Assessment in the Science Classroom*

### Multimedia Options

_____ **Videotape:** *MindJogger Videoquizzes*

_____ **Videotape:** *The Mechanical Universe,* Quad 4

_____ **Videodisc:** *STVS* Physics, Disc 1, Side 1, Ch. 5; Side 2, Chs. 6–10

_____ **Software:** *Computer Test Bank*

Date _____ Period _____ Name _____

**KEY**
*SE* = Student Edition, *TWE* = Teacher Wraparound Edition, *TCR* = Teacher Classroom Resources, *STVS* = Science and Technology Videodisc Series, *PCA* = Physics for the Computer Age

# 13.2 Lesson Plans

## The Solid State

### Section Objectives

_____ **Compare** solids, liquids, gases, and plasmas at a microscopic level, and **relate** their properties to their structures.

_____ **Explain** why solids expand and contract when the temperature changes.

_____ **Calculate** the expansion of solids and **discuss** the problems caused by expansion.

**National Science Content Standards** UCP.1, UCP.2, UCP.3, UCP.5; A.1, B.2, B.6, E.1, E.2

**Schedule**

Block schedule: 1 1/2 sessions
Single-period schedule: 3 sessions

### Focus

_____ Quick Demo, *TWE* p. 314

### Teach

_____ Physics & Technology, *SE* p. 316
_____ Pocket Lab, *SE* p. 317
_____ Help Wanted, *SE* p. 319
_____ Quick Demos, *TWE* pp. 315, 319
_____ Connections to Biology, *TWE* p. 316

_____ Demonstration 13-2, *TWE* p. 317
_____ Applying Physics, *TWE* pp. 319, 320
_____ Physics Journal, *TWE* p. 320
_____ *Physics Lab and Pocket Lab Worksheets*, p. 67, *TCR*
_____ *Spanish Resources, TCR*

### Assess/Reteach

_____ Section Review, *SE* p. 321
_____ Checking for Understanding, *TWE* p. 321
_____ Reteaching, *TWE* p. 321

_____ *Study Guide*, pp. 77–78, *TCR*
_____ *Supplemental Problems, TCR*

### Enrichment/Application

_____ Extension, *TWE* p. 321

_____ *Critical Thinking*, p. 19, *TCR*

### Close

_____ Closing Strategy, *TWE* p. 321

### Chapter Assessment

_____ Chapter Review, *SE* pp. 322–325
_____ Assessment, *TWE* pp. 317, 318
_____ Chapter Assessment, pp. 59–64, *TCR*

_____ *Alternate Assessment in the Science Classroom*
_____ *Performance Assessment in the Science Classroom*

### Multimedia Options

_____ **Videotape:** *MindJogger Videoquizzes*
_____ **Videodisc:** *STVS* Earth and Space Disc 3, Side 2, Ch. 16

_____ **Software:** *Computer Test Bank*

# 14.1 Lesson Plans

## Wave Properties

### Section Objectives

_____ **Identify** how waves transfer energy without transferring matter.

_____ **Contrast** transverse and longitudinal waves.

_____ **Relate** wave speed, wavelength, and frequency.

**National Science Content Standards** UCP.2, UCP.3, UCP.5; A.1, A.2, B.4, B.5, B.6, D.1, F.5

**Schedule**

Block schedule: 1 session

Single-period schedule: 2 sessions

### Focus

_____ Quick Demo, *TWE* p. 328

### Teach

_____ Design Your Own Physics Lab, *SE* p. 330

_____ Help Wanted, *SE* p. 332

_____ Physics & Society, *SE* p. 334

_____ Earth Science Connection, *SE* p. 335

_____ Quick Demos, *TWE* pp. 327, 331

_____ Physics Journal, *TWE* p. 329

_____ Connections to Architecture, *TWE* p. 331

_____ Demonstration 14-1, *TWE* pp. 332–333

_____ Applying Physics, *TWE* p. 332

_____ Transparency 21 Master and Worksheet, pp. 43–44, *TCR*

_____ *Physics Lab and Pocket Lab Worksheets*, pp. 69–70, *TCR*

_____ *Laboratory Manual*, Lab 14.2, *TCR*

_____ *Spanish Resources*, *TCR*

### Assess/Reteach

_____ Section Review, *SE* p. 335

_____ Checking for Understanding, *TWE* p. 335

_____ Reteaching, *TWE* p. 335

_____ *Study Guide*, pp. 79–82, *TCR*

_____ *Reteaching*, p. 19, *TCR*

_____ *Supplemental Problems*, *TCR*

### Enrichment/Application

_____ Cultural Diversity, TWE p. 331

_____ Enrichment, TWE pp. 332, 333

_____ Extension, TWE p. 335

_____ *Enrichment*, pp. 27–28, *TCR*

### Close

_____ Convergent Question, *TWE* p. 335

### Chapter Assessment

_____ Assessment, *TWE* p. 332

_____ *Alternate Assessment in the Science Classroom*

_____ *Performance Assessment in the Science Classroom*

### Multimedia Options

_____ **CD-ROM:** Waves, *PCA*

_____ **Videotape:** *MindJogger Videoquizzes*

_____ **Videotape:** *The Mechanical Universe*, Quad 4

_____ **Videodisc:** *STVS* Earth and Space Disc 3, Side 2, Chs. 12, 13; Physics Disc 1, Side 1, Ch. 6

_____ **Software:** *Computer Test Bank*

# 14.2 Lesson Plans

**KEY**
*SE* = Student Edition, *TWE* = Teacher Wraparound Edition, *TCR* = Teacher Classroom Resources, *STVS* = Science and Technology Videodisc Series, *PCA* = Physics for the Computer Age

## Wave Behavior

### Section Objectives

_____ **Relate** a wave's speed to the medium in which the wave travels.

_____ **Describe** how waves are reflected and refracted at boundaries between media and **explain** how waves diffract.

_____ **Apply** the principle of superposition to the phenomenon of interference.

**National Science Content Standards** UCP.2, UCP.3; B.4, B.6, D.1

**Schedule**

Block schedule: 2 1/2 sessions

Single-period schedule: 4 sessions

### Focus

_____ Quick Demo, *TWE* p. 336

### Teach

_____ Pocket Labs, *SE* pp. 337, 339, 340

_____ Physics Journal, *TWE* p. 337

_____ Quick Demos, *TWE* pp. 338, 342

_____ Demonstration 14-2, *TWE* pp. 338–339

_____ Demonstration 14-3, *TWE* pp. 340–341

_____ Applying Physics, *TWE* p. 342

_____ Tech Prep, *TWE* p. 342

_____ *Physics Lab and Pocket Lab Worksheets, pp. 71–73, TCR*

_____ *Laboratory Manual,* Lab 14.1, *TCR*

_____ *Graphing Calculators in the Science Classroom*

_____ *Spanish Resources, TCR*

### Assess/Reteach

_____ Section Review, *SE* p. 343

_____ Checking for Understanding, *TWE* p. 343

_____ Reteaching, *TWE* p. 343

_____ *Study Guide,* pp. 83–84, *TCR*

_____ *Supplemental Problems, TCR*

### Enrichment/Application

_____ Extension, *TWE* p. 343

_____ *Critical Thinking,* p. 20, *TCR*

### Close

_____ Closing Strategy, *TWE* p. 343

### Chapter Assessment

_____ Chapter Review, *SE* pp. 344–347

_____ Assessment, *TWE* p. 341

_____ *Chapter Assessment,* pp. 65–68, *TCR*

_____ *Alternate Assessment in the Science Classroom*

_____ *Performance Assessment in the Science Classroom*

### Multimedia Options

_____ **CD-ROM:** Introduction, *PCA*

_____ **Videotape:** *MindJogger Videoquizzes*

_____ **Videodisc:** *STVS* Earth and Space Disc 3, Side 2, Ch. 20; Physics Disc 1, Side 1, Ch. 5

_____ **Software:** *Computer Test Bank*

# 15.1 Lesson Plans

## Properties of Sound

### Section Objectives

_____ **Demonstrate** knowledge of the nature of sound waves and the properties sound shares with other waves.

_____ **Solve** problems relating the frequency, wavelength, and velocity of sound.

_____ **Relate** the physical properties of sound waves to the way we perceive sound.

_____ **Define** the Doppler shift and **identify** some of its applications.

**National Science Content Standards** UCP.2, UCP.3; A.2, B.2, B.6, C.6, G.1

**Schedule**

Block schedule: 1 1/2 sessions
Single-period schedule: 2 sessions

### Focus

_____ Discrepant Event, *TWE* p. 350

### Teach

_____ Help Wanted, *SE* p. 352
_____ Physics & Society, *SE* p. 356
_____ Quick Demos, *TWE* pp. 349, 353
_____ Applying Physics, *TWE* p. 351
_____ Tech Prep, *TWE* p. 352
_____ Demonstration 15-1, *TWE* p. 352

_____ Physics Journal, *TWE* p. 353
_____ Connections to History, *TWE* p. 354
_____ Transparencies 22, 23 Masters and Worksheets, pp. 45–48, *TCR*
_____ *Laboratory Manual*, Lab 15.1, *TCR*
_____ *Spanish Resources*, *TCR*

### Assess/Reteach

_____ Section Review, *SE* p. 355
_____ Checking for Understanding, *TWE* p. 355
_____ Reteaching, *TWE* p. 355

_____ Study Guide, pp. 85–88, *TCR*
_____ *Supplemental Problems*, *TCR*

### Enrichment/Application

_____ Cultural Diversity, *TWE* p. 353
_____ Enrichment, *TWE* p. 354

_____ Extension, *TWE* p. 355

### Close

_____ Convergent Question, *TWE* p. 355

### Chapter Assessment

_____ Assessment, *TWE* p. 354
_____ *Alternate Assessment in the Science Classroom*

_____ *Performance Assessment in the Science Classroom*

### Multimedia Options

_____ **Videotape:** *MindJogger Videoquizzes*
_____ **Videodisc:** *STVS* Physics Disc 1, Side 1, Chs. 7, 11, 17

_____ **Software:** *Computer Test Bank*

# 15.2 Lesson Plans

**KEY**
*SE* = Student Edition, *TWE* = Teacher
Wraparound Edition, *TCR* = Teacher
Classroom Resources, *STVS* = Science
and Technology Videodisc Series,
*PCA* = Physics for the Computer Age

## The Physics of Music

### Section Objectives

_____ **Describe** the origin of sound.

_____ **Demonstrate** an understanding of resonance, especially as applied to air columns.

_____ **Explain** why there is a variation among instruments and among voices using the terms *timbre*, *resonance*, *fundamental*, and *harmonic*.

_____ **Determine** why beats occur.

**National Science Content Standards** UCP.2, UCP.3, UCP.5; A.1, A.2, B.6, C.5, E.1, E.2, G.1, G.2, G.3

**Schedule**

Block schedule: 1 1/2 sessions

Single-period schedule: 3 sessions

### Focus

▭ Activity, *TWE* p. 358

### Teach

▭ Pocket Labs, *SE* pp. 360, 365

▭ Physics Lab, *SE* p. 362

_____ Biology Connection, *SE* p. 363

▭ Demonstration 15-2, *TWE* pp. 358–359

▭ Demonstration 15-3, *TWE* pp. 364–365

▭ Demonstration 15-4, *TWE* p. 366

▭ Quick Demos, *TWE* pp. 359, 361, 363

_____ Connections to Biology, *TWE* p. 363

_____ Tech Prep, *TWE* p. 365

_____ Physics Journal, *TWE* p. 366

▭ Transparency 24 Master and Worksheet, pp. 49–50, *TCR*

▭ *Laboratory Manual*, Lab 15.2, *TCR*

▭ *Physics Lab and Pocket Lab Worksheets*, pp. 75–78, *TCR*

_____ *Spanish Resources*, *TCR*

### Assess/Reteach

▭ Section Review, *SE* p. 367

_____ Checking for Understanding, *TWE* p. 367

▭ Reteaching, *TWE* p. 367

▭ *Study Guide*, pp. 89–90, *TCR*

▭ *Reteaching*, p. 20, *TCR*

_____ *Supplemental Problems*, *TCR*

### Enrichment/Application

_____ Enrichment, *TWE* p. 361

_____ Cultural Diversity, *TWE* p. 361

▭ Extension, *TWE* p. 367

_____ *Enrichment*, pp. 29–30, *TCR*

_____ *Critical Thinking*, p. 21, *TCR*

▭ *Tech Prep Applications*, pp. 23–26, *TCR*

### Close

▭ Closing Strategy, *TWE* p. 367

### Chapter Assessment

▭ Chapter Review, *SE* pp. 368–371

_____ Assessment, *TWE* pp. 360, 366

▭ *Chapter Assessment*, pp. 69–72, *TCR*

_____ *Alternate Assessment in the Science Classroom*

_____ *Performance Assessment in the Science Classroom*

### Multimedia Options

▭ **Videotape:** *MindJogger Videoquizzes*

_____ **Software:** *Computer Test Bank*

# 16.1 Lesson Plans

## Light Fundamentals

### Section Objectives

_____ **Recognize** that light is the visible portion of an entire range of electromagnetic frequencies.
_____ **Describe** the ray model of light.
_____ **Solve** problems involving the speed of light.
_____ **Define** *luminous intensity*, *luminous flux*, and *illuminance*.
_____ **Solve** illumination problems.

**National Science Content Standards** UCP.2, UCP.3, UCP.5; A.1, A.2, B.6, E.1, G.1, G.2, G.3
**Schedule**
Block schedule: 1 1/2 sessions
Single-period schedule: 2 sessions

### Focus

_____ Focus Strategy, *TWE* p. 374

### Teach

_____ Help Wanted, *SE* p. 376
_____ Physics Lab, *SE* p. 377
_____ Physics & Technology, *SE* p. 378
_____ Pocket Lab, *SE* p. 380
_____ Quick Demos, *TWE* pp. 373, 375
_____ Physics Journal, *TWE* p. 375
_____ Demonstration 16-1, *TWE* pp. 378–379

_____ Applying Physics, *TWE* p. 379
_____ Tech Prep, *TWE* p. 381
_____ *Graphing Calculators in the Science Classroom*
_____ *Physics Lab and Pocket Lab Worksheets*, pp. 79–81, *TCR*
_____ *Laboratory Manual*, Lab 16.2, *TCR*
_____ *Spanish Resources*, *TCR*

### Assess/Reteach

_____ Section Review, *SE* p. 381
_____ Checking for Understanding, *TWE* p. 381
_____ Reteaching, *TWE* p. 381

_____ *Study Guide*, pp. 91–93, *TCR*
_____ *Supplemental Problems*, *TCR*

### Enrichment/Application

_____ Enrichment, *TWE* pp. 376, 378, 379
_____ Cultural Diversity, *TWE* p. 376
_____ Extension, *TWE* p. 381

_____ *Critical Thinking*, p. 22, *TCR*
_____ *Enrichment*, pp. 31–32, *TCR*

### Close

_____ Closing Strategy, *TWE* p. 381

### Chapter Assessment

_____ Assessment, *TWE* p. 379
_____ *Alternate Assessment in the Science Classroom*

_____ *Performance Assessment in the Science Classroom*

### Multimedia Options

_____ **Videotape:** *MindJogger Videoquizzes*
_____ **Videodisc:** *STVS* Physics, Disc 1, Side 1, Ch. 9

_____ **Software:** *Computer Test Bank*

# 16.2 Lesson Plans

## Light and Matter

### Section Objectives

_____ **Explain** the formation of color by light and by pigments or dyes.

_____ **Explain** the cause and **give examples** of interference in thin films.

_____ **Describe** methods of producing polarized light.

**National Science Content Standards** UCP.2, UCP.3; A.2, B.2, G.1, G.2, G.3

**Schedule**

Block schedule: 1 1/2 sessions

Single-period schedule: 3 sessions

### Focus

_____ Focus Strategy, *TWE* p. 382

### Teach

_____ Pocket Labs, *SE* pp. 383, 386, 387

_____ Quick Demos, *TWE* pp. 382, 385

_____ Physics Journal, *TWE* pp. 384, 385

_____ Connections to Biology, *TWE* p. 384

_____ Demonstration 16-2, *TWE* pp. 386–387

_____ Applying Physics, *TWE* p. 387

_____ Transparencies 25, 26, 27 Masters and Worksheets, pp. 51–56, *TCR*

_____ *Physics Lab and Pocket Lab Worksheets, pp. 82–84, TCR*

_____ *Laboratory Manual,* Lab 16.1, *TCR*

_____ *Spanish Resources, TCR*

### Assess/Reteach

_____ Section Review, *SE* p. 388

_____ Checking for Understanding, *TWE* p. 388

_____ Reteaching, *TWE* p. 388

_____ *Study Guide,* pp. 94–95, *TCR*

_____ *Reteaching,* p. 21, *TCR*

_____ *Supplemental Problems, TCR*

### Enrichment/Application

_____ Enrichment, *TWE* p. 386

_____ Extension, *TWE* p. 388

### Close

_____ Closing Strategy, *TWE* p. 388

### Chapter Assessment

_____ Chapter Review, *SE* pp. 389–391

_____ Assessment, *TWE* p. 385

_____ *Chapter Assessment,* pp. 73–76, *TCR*

_____ *Alternate Assessment in the Science Classroom*

_____ *Performance Assessment in the Science Classroom*

### Multimedia Options

_____ **CD-ROM:** Waves, *PCA*

_____ **Videotape:** *MindJogger Videoquizzes*

_____ **Videotape:** *The Mechanical Universe,* Quad 7

_____ **Videodisc:** *STVS* Physics, Disc 1, Side 1, Ch. 10; Disc 1, Side 2, Ch. 22

_____ **Software:** *Computer Test Bank*

# 17.1 Lesson Plans

**KEY**
*SE* = Student Edition, *TWE* = Teacher Wraparound Edition, *TCR* = Teacher Classroom Resources, *STVS* = Science and Technology Videodisc Series, *PCA* = Physics for the Computer Age

## How Light Behaves at a Boundary

### Section Objectives

_____ **Explain** the law of reflection.
_____ **Distinguish** between diffuse and regular reflection and **provide** examples.
_____ **Calculate** the index of refraction in a medium.

**National Science Content Standards** UCP.2, UCP.3, UCP.5; A.1, A.2, B.2, B.6, G.3

**Schedule**
Block schedule: 2 sessions
Single-period schedule: 3 sessions

### Focus

_____ Activity, *TWE* p. 395

### Teach

_____ Pocket Labs, *SE* pp. 394, 400
_____ Physics Lab, *SE* p. 399
_____ Help Wanted, *SE* p. 402
_____ Quick Demos, *TWE* pp. 393, 398
_____ Physics Journal, *TWE* pp. 395, 401
_____ Demonstration 17-1, *TWE* p. 396
_____ Demonstration 17-2, *TWE* pp. 400–401
_____ Applying Physics, *TWE* p. 397

_____ Connections to Chemistry, *TWE* p. 397
_____ Connections to History, *TWE* p. 398
_____ Transparency 28 Master and Worksheet, pp. 57–58, *TCR*
_____ *Physics Lab and Pocket Lab Worksheets, pp. 85–88, TCR*
_____ *Laboratory Manual*, Labs 17.1, 17.2, *TCR*
_____ *Spanish Resources, TCR*

### Assess/Reteach

_____ Section Review, *SE* p. 402
_____ Checking for Understanding, *TWE* p. 401
_____ Reteaching, *TWE* p. 401

_____ *Study Guide*, pp. 97–100, *TCR*
_____ *Reteaching*, p. 22, *TCR*
_____ *Supplemental Problems, TCR*

### Enrichment/Application

_____ Enrichment, *TWE* p. 398
_____ Extension, *TWE* p. 401

_____ *Enrichment*, pp. 33–34, *TCR*

### Close

_____ Quick Demo, *TWE* p. 402

### Chapter Assessment

_____ Assessment, *TWE* p. 397
_____ *Alternate Assessment in the Science Classroom*

_____ *Performance Assessment in the Science Classroom*

### Multimedia Options

_____ **Videotape:** *MindJogger Videoquizzes*
_____ **Videotape:** *The Mechanical Universe*, Quad 7

_____ **Videodisc:** *STVS* Physics, Disc 1, Side 1, Ch. 7; Disc 1, Side 2, Ch. 11
_____ **Software:** *Computer Test Bank*

# 17.2 Lesson Plans

**KEY**
*SE* = Student Edition, *TWE* = Teacher Wraparound Edition, *TCR* = Teacher Classroom Resources, *STVS* = Science and Technology Videodisc Series, *PCA* = Physics for the Computer Age

## Applications of Reflected and Refracted Light

### Section Objectives

_____ **Explain** total internal reflection.
_____ **Define** the critical angle.
_____ **Explain** effects caused by the refraction of light in a medium with varying refractive indices.
_____ **Explain** dispersion of light in terms of the index of refraction.

**National Science Content Standards** UCP.2, UCP.5; A.2, B.6, E.1, E.2, F.6
**Schedule**
Block schedule: 1 1/2 sessions
Single-period schedule: 3 sessions

### Focus

_____ Activity, *TWE* p. 403

### Teach

_____ Pocket Labs, *SE* pp. 404, 408
_____ How It Works, *SE* p. 405
_____ Literature Connection, *SE* p. 407
_____ Demonstration 17-3, *TWE* pp. 404–405
_____ Quick Demos, *TWE* pp. 406, 408
_____ Physics Journal, *TWE* p. 406

_____ Tech Prep, *TWE* p. 407
_____ Connections to Computer Science, *TWE* p. 408
_____ *Physics Lab and Pocket Lab Worksheets, pp. 89–90, TCR*
_____ *Spanish Resources, TCR*

### Assess/Reteach

_____ Section Review, *SE* p. 409
_____ Checking for Understanding, *TWE* p. 409
_____ Reteaching, *TWE* p. 409

_____ *Study Guide, pp. 101–102, TCR*
_____ *Supplemental Problems, TCR*

### Enrichment/Application

_____ Cultural Diversity, *TWE* p. 406
_____ Extension, *TWE* p. 409

_____ *Critical Thinking, p. 23, TCR*

### Close

_____ Convergent Question, *TWE* p. 409

### Chapter Assessment

_____ Chapter Review, *SE* pp. 410–413
_____ Assessment, *TWE* p. 407
_____ *Chapter Assessment, pp. 77–80, TCR*

_____ *Alternate Assessment in the Science Classroom*
_____ *Performance Assessment in the Science Classroom*

### Multimedia Options

_____ **Videotape:** *MindJogger Videoquizzes*
_____ **Videodisc:** *STVS* Physics, Disc 1, Side 1, Chs. 10, 16

_____ **Software:** *Computer Test Bank*

# 18.1 Lesson Plans

## Mirrors

### Section Objectives

_____ **Explain** how concave, convex, and plane mirrors form images.

_____ **Locate** images using ray diagrams, and **calculate** image location and size using equations.

_____ **Explain** the cause of spherical aberration and how the effect may be overcome.

_____ **Describe** uses of parabolic mirrors.

**National Science Content Standards** UCP.2, UCP.3, UCP.5; A.2, B.6, E.1, F.6, G.1

### Schedule

Block schedule: 1 session

Single-period schedule: 2 sessions

### Focus

_____ Activity, *TWE* p. 416

### Teach

_____ Pocket Labs, *SE* pp. 417, 418, 419, 420, 425

_____ Help Wanted, *SE* p. 421

_____ Physics & Technology, *SE* p. 428

_____ Quick Demos, *TWE* pp. 415, 417, 419

_____ Applying Physics, *TWE* pp. 418, 426

_____ Demonstration 18-1, *TWE* pp. 418–419

_____ Demonstration 18-2, *TWE* pp. 422–423

_____ Connections to History, *TWE* pp. 420, 424

_____ Tech Prep, *TWE* p. 427

_____ Transparency 29 Master and Worksheet, pp. 59–61, *TCR*

_____ *Physics Lab and Pocket Lab Worksheets*, pp. 93–97, TCR

_____ *Laboratory Manual*, Lab 18.1, *TCR*

_____ *Graphing Calculators in the Science Classroom*

_____ *Spanish Resources, TCR*

### Assess/Reteach

_____ Section Review, *SE* p. 428

_____ Checking for Understanding, *TWE* p. 427

_____ Reteaching, *TWE* p. 427

_____ *Study Guide*, pp. 103–105, *TCR*

_____ *Supplemental Problems, TCR*

### Enrichment/Application

_____ Cultural Diversity, *TWE* p. 421

_____ Enrichment, *TWE* pp. 423, 424, 426

_____ Extension, *TWE* p. 427

_____ *Tech Prep Applications*, pp. 27–30, *TCR*

### Close

_____ Convergent Question, *TWE* p. 427

### Chapter Assessment

_____ Assessments, *TWE* pp. 420, 423

_____ *Alternate Assessment in the Science Classroom*

_____ *Performance Assessment in the Science Classroom*

### Multimedia Options

_____ **Videotape:** *MindJogger Videoquizzes*

_____ **Videodisc:** *STVS* Chemistry, Disc 2, Side 2, Ch. 13; Earth and Space, Disc 3, Side 1, Ch. 8; Physics, Disc 1, Side 1, Ch. 9; Disc 1, Side 2, Ch. 17

_____ **Software:** *Computer Test Bank*

# 18.2 Lesson Plans

**KEY**
*SE* = Student Edition, *TWE* = Teacher Wraparound Edition, *TCR* = Teacher Classroom Resources, *STVS* = Science and Technology Videodisc Series, *PCA* = Physics for the Computer Age

## Lenses

### Section Objectives

_____ **Describe** how real and virtual images are formed by convex and concave lenses.

_____ **Locate** the image with a ray diagram and find the image location and size using a mathematical model.

_____ **Define** chromatic aberration and **explain** how it can be reduced.

_____ **Explain** how optical instruments such as microscopes and telescopes work.

**National Science Content Standards** UCP.2, UCP.3, UCP.5; A.1, A.2, B.6, C.5, E.1, E.2, F.1, G.1, G.3
**Schedule**
Block schedule: 2 1/2 sessions
Single-period schedule: 4 sessions

### Focus
_____ Activity, *TWE* p. 429

### Teach
_____ Pocket Labs, *SE* pp. 432, 435
_____ Physics Lab, *SE* p. 433
_____ Physics Journal, *TWE* p. 430
_____ Applying Physics, *TWE* pp. 431, 434
_____ Tech Prep, *TWE* p. 431
_____ Demonstration 18-3, *TWE* p. 432
_____ Connections to Law, *TWE* p. 435
_____ Connections to Medicine, *TWE* p. 437

_____ Quick Demo, *TWE* p. 436
_____ Transparencies 29, 30 Masters and Worksheets, pp. 59–64, *TCR*
_____ *Physics Lab and Pocket Lab Worksheets,* pp. 91–92, 98–99, *TCR*
_____ *Laboratory Manual,* Lab 18.2, *TCR*
_____ *Spanish Resources, TCR*

### Assess/Reteach
_____ Section Review, *SE* p. 438
_____ Checking for Understanding, *TWE* p. 437
_____ Reteaching, *TWE* p. 438

_____ *Study Guide,* pp. 106–108, *TCR*
_____ *Reteaching,* p. 23, *TCR*
_____ *Supplemental Problems, TCR*

### Enrichment/Application
_____ Enrichment, *TWE* pp. 430, 437
_____ Cultural Diversity, *TWE* p. 434
_____ Extension, *TWE* p. 438

_____ *Critical Thinking,* p. 24, *TCR*
_____ *Enrichment,* pp. 35–36, *TCR*

### Close
_____ Convergent Question, *TWE* p. 438

### Chapter Assessment
_____ Chapter Review, *SE* pp. 439–441
_____ Assessment, *TWE* p. 436
_____ *Chapter Assessment,* pp. 81–86, *TCR*

_____ *Alternate Assessment in the Science Classroom*
_____ *Performance Assessment in the Science Classroom*

### Multimedia Options
_____ **Videotape:** *MindJogger Videoquizzes*
_____ **Videodisc:** *STVS Physics,* Disc 1, Side 2, Ch. 13

_____ **Software:** *Computer Test Bank*

# 19.1 Lesson Plans

## When Light Waves Interfere

### Section Objectives

_____ **Relate** the diffraction of light to its wave characteristics.

_____ **Explain** how light falling on two closely spaced slits produces an interference pattern, and use measurements to **calculate** wavelengths of light.

_____ **Apply** geometrical models to **explain** single-slit diffraction and two-slit interference patterns.

**National Science Content Standards** UCP.2, UCP.3; A.1, A.2, B.6, G.1, G.2, G.3

**Schedule**

Block schedule: 1 session

Single-period schedule: 2 sessions

### Focus

_____ Activity, TWE p. 444

### Teach

_____ Physics Lab, SE p. 446

_____ Pocket Labs, SE pp. 447, 450

_____ Quick Demos, TWE pp. 443, 445, 448

_____ Physics Journal, TWE p. 445

_____ Connections to Biology, TWE p. 447

_____ Applying Physics, TWE p. 448

_____ Demonstration 19-1, TWE pp. 448–449

_____ Transparencies 31, 32 Masters and Worksheets, pp. 65–69, TCR

_____ Physics Lab and Pocket Lab Worksheets, pp. 101–104, TCR

_____ Laboratory Manual, Lab 19.1, TCR

_____ Spanish Resources, TCR

### Assess/Reteach

_____ Section Review, SE p. 451

_____ Checking for Understanding, TWE p. 450

_____ Reteaching, TWE p. 451

_____ Study Guide, pp. 109–112, TCR

_____ Supplemental Problems, TCR

### Enrichment/Application

_____ Cultural Diversity, TWE p. 445

_____ Enrichment, TWE p. 449

_____ Extension, TWE p. 451

_____ Enrichment, pp. 37–38, TCR

_____ Tech Prep Applications, pp. 31–32, TCR

_____ Critical Thinking, p. 25, TCR

### Close

_____ Closing Strategy, TWE p. 451

### Chapter Assessment

_____ Assessment, TWE p. 449

_____ Alternate Assessment in the Science Classroom

_____ Performance Assessment in the Science Classroom

### Multimedia Options

_____ CD-ROM: Waves, PCA

_____ Videotape: MindJogger Videoquizzes

_____ Videotape: The Mechanical Universe, Quad 7

_____ Software: Computer Test Bank

# 19.2 Lesson Plans

## Applications of Diffraction

### Section Objectives

_____ **Explain** how diffraction gratings form interference patterns and how they are used in grating spectrometers.

_____ **Discuss** how diffraction limits the ability of a lens to distinguish two closely spaced objects.

**National Science Content Standards** UCP.2, UCP.3, UCP.5; B.6, E.1, E.2, G.1, G.2, G.3

**Schedule**

Block schedule: 1 1/2 sessions

Single-period schedule: 2 sessions

### Focus

_____ Activity, *TWE* p. 452

### Teach

_____ How It Works, *SE* p. 453

_____ Help Wanted, *SE* p. 454

_____ Pocket Lab, *SE* p. 455

_____ Tech Prep, *TWE* p. 453

_____ Demonstration 19-2, *TWE* pp. 454–455

_____ Physics Journal, *TWE* p. 454

_____ Quick Demo, *TWE* p. 454

_____ *Physics Lab and Pocket Lab Worksheets,* p. 105, *TCR*

_____ *Laboratory Manual,* Lab 19.2, *TCR*

_____ *Spanish Resources, TCR*

### Assess/Reteach

_____ Section Review, *SE* p. 456

_____ Checking for Understanding, *TWE* p. 456

_____ Reteaching, *TWE* p. 456

_____ *Study Guide,* pp. 113–114, *TCR*

_____ *Reteaching,* p. 24, *TCR*

_____ *Supplemental Problems, TCR*

### Enrichment/Application

_____ Extension, *TWE* p. 456

### Close

_____ Closing Strategy, *TWE* p. 456

### Chapter Assessment

_____ Chapter Review, *SE* pp. 457–459

_____ Assessment, *TWE* pp. 455, 456

_____ *Chapter Assessment,* pp. 87–92, *TCR*

_____ *Alternate Assessment in the Science Classroom*

_____ *Performance Assessment in the Science Classroom*

### Multimedia Options

_____ **CD-ROM:** Diffraction and Interference of Waves, *PCA*

_____ **Videotape:** *MindJogger Videoquizzes*

_____ **Software:** *Computer Test Bank*

# 20.1 Lesson Plans

**KEY**
*SE* = Student Edition, *TWE* = Teacher Wraparound Edition, *TCR* = Teacher Classroom Resources, *STVS* = Science and Technology Videodisc Series, *PCA* = Physics for the Computer Age

## Electrical Charge

### Section Objectives

_____ **Recognize** that objects that are charged exert forces, both attractive and repulsive.

_____ **Demonstrate** that charging is the separation, not the creation, of electrical charges.

_____ **Describe** the differences between conductors and insulators.

**National Science Content Standards** UCP.2, UCP.3, UCP.4; A.1, A.2, B.1, E.2, G.1, G.2

**Schedule**

Block schedule: 1 session

Single-period schedule: 2 sessions

### Focus

_____ Activity, *TWE* p. 462

### Teach

_____ Help Wanted, *SE* p. 464

_____ Physics Lab, *SE* p. 467

_____ Quick Demos, *TWE* pp. 461, 464

_____ Demonstration 20-1, *TWE* p. 464

_____ Physics Journal, *TWE* p. 464

_____ Applying Physics, *TWE* p. 465

_____ Connections to Earth Science, *TWE* p. 465

_____ *Physics Lab and Pocket Lab Worksheets,* pp. 107–108, *TCR*

_____ *Graphing Calculators in the Science Classroom*

_____ *Spanish Resources, TCR*

### Assess/Reteach

_____ Section Review, *SE* p. 466

_____ Checking for Understanding, *TWE* p. 465

_____ Reteaching, *TWE* p. 466

_____ *Study Guide,* pp. 115–116, *TCR*

_____ *Supplemental Problems, TCR*

### Enrichment/Application

_____ Enrichment, *TWE* p. 465

_____ Extension, *TWE* p. 466

### Close

_____ Activity, *TWE* p. 466

### Chapter Assessment

_____ Assessment, *TWE* p. 463

_____ *Alternate Assessment in the Science Classroom*

_____ *Performance Assessment in the Science Classroom*

### Multimedia Options

_____ **CD-ROM:** *Interactive Physics*

_____ **Videotape:** *MindJogger Videoquizzes*

_____ **Software:** *Computer Test Bank*

# 20.2 Lesson Plans

## Electrical Force

### Section Objectives

_____ **Summarize** the relationship between forces and charges.

_____ **Describe** how an electroscope detects electric charge.

_____ **Explain** how to charge by conduction and induction.

_____ **Use** Coulomb's law to **solve** problems relating to electrical force.

_____ **Develop** a model of how charged objects can attract a neutral object.

**National Science Content Standards** UCP.2, UCP.3, UCP.5; A.2, B.4, D.1, E.1, E.2, F.4, F.6, G.1, G.2, G.3

**Schedule**

Block schedule: 2 1/2 sessions

Single-period schedule: 4 sessions

### Focus

_____ Discrepant Event, *TWE* p. 468

### Teach

_____ Pocket Labs, *SE* pp. 471, 472

_____ How It Works, *SE* p. 473

_____ Quick Demos, *TWE* pp. 469, 470

_____ Connections to Chemistry, *TWE* p. 469

_____ Demonstration 20-2, *TWE* pp. 470–471

_____ Physics Journal, *TWE* p. 474

_____ Tech Prep, *TWE* p. 474

_____ Transparencies 33, 34 Masters and Worksheets, pp. 71–74, *TCR*

_____ *Physics Lab and Pocket Lab Worksheets,* pp. 109–110, *TCR*

_____ *Laboratory Manual,* Lab 20.1, *TCR*

_____ *Spanish Resources, TCR*

### Assess/Reteach

_____ Section Review, *SE* p. 476

_____ Checking for Understanding, *TWE* p. 475

_____ Reteaching, *TWE* p. 475

_____ *Study Guide,* pp. 117–120, *TCR*

_____ *Reteaching,* p. 25, *TCR*

_____ *Supplemental Problems, TCR*

### Enrichment/Application

_____ Cultural Diversity, *TWE* p. 472

_____ Enrichment, *TWE* p. 474

_____ Extension, *TWE* p. 475

_____ *Critical Thinking,* p. 26, *TCR*

_____ *Enrichment,* p. 39, *TCR*

### Close

_____ Activity, *TWE* p. 476

### Chapter Assessment

_____ Chapter Review, *SE* pp. 477–479

_____ Assessment, *TWE* p. 472

_____ *Chapter Assessment,* pp. 93–98, *TCR*

_____ *Alternate Assessment in the Science Classroom*

_____ *Performance Assessment in the Science Classroom*

### Multimedia Options

_____ **Videotape:** *MindJogger Videoquizzes*

_____ **Videotape:** *The Mechanical Universe,* Quad 5

_____ **Videodisc:** *STVS Physics,* Disc 1, Side 1, Ch. 18

_____ **Software:** *Computer Test Bank*

# 21.1 Lesson Plans

## Creating and Measuring Electric Fields

### Section Objectives

_____ **Define** and **measure** an electric field.
_____ **Solve** problems relating to charge, electric fields, and forces.
_____ **Diagram** electric field lines.

**National Science Content Standards** UCP.1, UCP.2, UCP.3; A.1, A.2, B.4
**Schedule**
Block schedule: 1 session
Single-period schedule: 2 sessions

### Focus

_____ Discrepant Event, *TWE* p. 482

### Teach

_____ Pocket Lab, *SE* p. 484
_____ Physics & Society, *SE* p. 486
_____ Quick Demos, *TWE* pp. 481, 483
_____ Demonstration 21-1, *TWE* pp. 484–485
_____ Physics Journal, *TWE* p. 485

_____ *Physics Lab and Pocket Lab Worksheets, p. 113, TCR*
_____ *Physics Skills, pp. 39–40, TCR*
_____ *Spanish Resources, TCR*

### Assess/Reteach

_____ Section Review, *SE* p. 487
_____ Checking for Understanding, *TWE* p. 487
_____ Reteaching, *TWE* p. 487

_____ *Study Guide, pp. 121–123, TCR*
_____ *Reteaching, pp. 26–27, TCR*
_____ *Supplemental Problems, TCR*

### Enrichment/Application

_____ Enrichment, *TWE* p. 483

_____ *Extension, TWE* p. 487

### Close

_____ Activity, *TWE* p. 487

### Chapter Assessment

_____ Assessment, *TWE* p. 485
_____ *Alternate Assessment in the Science Classroom*

_____ *Performance Assessment in the Science Classroom*

### Multimedia Options

_____ CD-ROM: *Interactive Physics*
_____ Videotape: *MindJogger Videoquizzes*

_____ **Software:** *Computer Test Bank*

# 21.2 Lesson Plans

## Applications of Electric Fields

### Section Objectives

_____ **Define** and **calculate** electric potential difference.

_____ **Explain** how Millikan used electric fields to find the charge of the electron.

_____ **Determine** where charges reside on solid and hollow conductors.

_____ **Describe** capacitance and **solve** capacitor problems.

**National Science Content Standards** UCP.1, UCP.2, UCP.3, UCP.5; A.2, B.1, B.4, C.6, D.1, E.1, E.2, F.1, G.1, G.2, G.3

**Schedule**

Block schedule: 2 sessions

Single-period schedule: 3 sessions

### Focus

_____ Discrepant Event, *TWE* p. 488

### Teach

_____ Help Wanted, *SE* p. 489

_____ Biology Connection, *SE* p. 493

_____ Physics Lab, *SE* p. 496

_____ Applying Physics, *TWE* pp. 490, 495

_____ Connections to Biology, *TWE* p. 490

_____ Physics Journal, *TWE* p. 492

_____ Quick Demos, *TWE* pp. 492, 497, 498, 499

_____ Tech Prep, *TWE* p. 494

_____ Demonstration 21-2, *TWE* pp. 498–499

_____ Transparencies 35, 36 Masters and Worksheets, pp. 75–78, *TCR*

_____ *Physics Lab and Pocket Lab Worksheets, pp. 111–112, TCR*

_____ *Laboratory Manual,* Lab 21.1, *TCR*

_____ *Spanish Resources, TCR*

### Assess/Reteach

_____ Section Review, *SE* p. 501

_____ Checking for Understanding, *TWE* p. 500

_____ Reteaching, *TWE* p. 500

_____ *Study Guide,* pp. 124–126, *TCR*

_____ *Supplemental Problems, TCR*

### Enrichment/Application

_____ Cultural Diversity, *TWE* p. 492

_____ Enrichment, *TWE* p. 494

_____ Extension, *TWE* p. 500

_____ *Critical Thinking,* p. 27, *TCR*

_____ *Enrichment,* pp. 41–42, *TCR*

### Close

_____ Activity, *TWE* p. 501

### Chapter Assessment

_____ Chapter Review, *SE* pp. 502–505

_____ Assessment, *TWE* p. 491, 500

_____ *Chapter Assessment,* pp. 99–102, *TCR*

_____ *Alternate Assessment in the Science Classroom*

_____ *Performance Assessment in the Science Classroom*

### Multimedia Options

_____ **Videotape:** *MindJogger Videoquizzes*

_____ **Videotape:** *The Mechanical Universe,* Quads 3, 5

_____ **Videodisc:** *STVS* Earth and Space, Disc 3, Side 1, Ch. 13

_____ **Software:** *Computer Test Bank*

# 22.1 Lesson Plans

**KEY**
*SE* = Student Edition, *TWE* = Teacher Wraparound Edition, *TCR* = Teacher Classroom Resources, *STVS* = Science and Technology Videodisc Series, *PCA* = Physics for the Computer Age

## Current and Circuits

### Section Objectives

_____ **Define** an electric current and the ampere.
_____ **Describe** conditions that create current in an electric circuit.
_____ **Draw** circuits and **recognize** that they are closed loops.
_____ **Define** power in electric circuits.
_____ **Define** *resistance* and **describe** Ohm's law.

**National Science Content Standards** UCP.1, UCP.2, UCP.3, UCP.4, UCP.5; A.1, A.2, B.5, C.6, E.1, E.2, F.1, F.5, G.2

**Schedule**
Block schedule: 2 sessions
Single-period schedule: 3 sessions

### Focus

_____ Activity, *TWE* p. 508

### Teach

_____ Help Wanted, *SE* p. 510
_____ Pocket Labs, *SE* pp. 512, 516
_____ Biology Connection, *SE* p. 515
_____ Physics Lab, *SE* p. 518
_____ Physics & Technology, *SE* p. 519
_____ Quick Demos, *TWE* pp. 507, 511
_____ Physics Journal, *TWE* p. 510
_____ Connections to Chemistry, *TWE* p. 511
_____ Tech Prep, *TWE* p. 513

_____ Connections to Engineering, *TWE* p. 514
_____ Demonstration 22-1, *TWE* pp. 516–517
_____ Transparencies 37, 38 Masters and Worksheets, pp. 79–82, *TCR*
_____ *Physics Lab and Pocket Lab Worksheets,* pp. 118–119, *TCR*
_____ *Laboratory Manual,* Lab 22.1, *TCR*
_____ *Spanish Resources, TCR*

### Assess/Reteach

_____ Section Review, *SE* p. 519
_____ Checking for Understanding, *TWE* p. 517
_____ Reteaching, *TWE* p. 517

_____ Study *Guide,* pp. 127–131, *TCR*
_____ *Reteaching,* p. 28, *TCR*
_____ *Supplemental Problems, TCR*

### Enrichment/Application

_____ Cultural Diversity, *TWE* p. 512
_____ Enrichment, *TWE* p. 515

_____ Extension, *TWE* p. 517
_____ *Enrichment,* pp. 43–44, *TCR*

### Close

_____ Closing Strategy, *TWE* p. 519

### Chapter Assessment

_____ Assessment, *TWE* pp. 512, 513, 514
_____ *Alternate Assessment in the Science Classroom*

_____ *Performance Assessment in the Science Classroom*

### Multimedia Options

_____ CD-ROM: Electricity, *PCA*
_____ Videotape: *MindJogger Videoquizzes*
_____ Videotape: *The Mechanical Universe,* Quad 5

_____ **Videodisc:** *STVS* Chemistry, Disc 2, Side 2, Chs. 8, 13, 14, 15, 16; Physics, Disc 1, Side 2, Ch. 14
_____ **Software:** *Computer Test Bank*

# 22.2 Lesson Plans

**KEY**
*SE* = Student Edition, *TWE* = Teacher Wraparound Edition, *TCR* = Teacher Classroom Resources, *STVS* = Science and Technology Videodisc Series, *PCA* = Physics for the Computer Age

## Using Electric Energy

### Section Objectives

_____ **Explain** how electric energy is converted into thermal energy.

_____ **Determine** why high-voltage transmission lines are used to carry electric energy over long distances.

_____ **Define** *kilowatt-hour*.

**National Science Content Standards** UCP.1, UCP.3, UCP.5; A.2, B.5, D.1, D.2, E.1, E.2, F.3

**Schedule**

Block schedule: 1 1/2 sessions

Single-period schedule: 3 sessions

### Focus

_____ Focus Strategy, *TWE* p. 520

### Teach

_____ Pocket Labs, *SE* pp. 521, 522

_____ Demonstration 22-2, *TWE* pp. 522–523

_____ Quick Demo, *TWE* p. 523

_____ Physics Journal, *TWE* p. 524

_____ *Graphing Calculators in the Science Classroom*

_____ *Physics Lab and Pocket Lab Worksheets*, pp. 120–121, *TCR*

_____ *Laboratory Manual*, Lab 22.2, *TCR*

_____ *Physics Skills*, Skill 19, pp. 39–40, *TCR*

_____ *Spanish Resources*, *TCR*

### Assess/Reteach

_____ Section Review, *SE* p. 525

_____ Checking for Understanding, *TWE* p. 524

_____ Reteaching, *TWE* p. 525

_____ *Study Guide*, p. 132, *TCR*

_____ *Supplemental Problems*, *TCR*

### Enrichment/Application

_____ Enrichment, *TWE* p. 522

_____ Extension, *TWE* p. 525

_____ *Tech Prep Applications*, pp. 33–34, *TCR*

_____ *Critical Thinking*, pp. 28–29, *TCR*

### Close

_____ Activity, *TWE* p. 525

### Chapter Assessment

_____ Chapter Review, *SE* pp. 526–529

_____ Assessment, *TWE* p. 525

_____ *Chapter Assessment*, pp. 103–106, *TCR*

_____ *Alternate Assessment in the Science Classroom*

_____ *Performance Assessment in the Science Classroom*

### Multimedia Options

_____ **Videotape:** *MindJogger Videoquizzes*

_____ **Software:** *Computer Test Bank*

# 23.1 Lesson Plans

## Simple Circuits

### Section Objectives

_____ **Describe** both a series connection and a parallel connection and **state** the important characteristics of each.

_____ **Calculate** current, voltage drops, and equivalent resistance for devices connected in series and in parallel.

_____ **Describe** a voltage divider and **solve** problems involving one.

**National Science Content Standards** UCP.1, UCP.2, UCP.3, UCP.5; A.2, E.1, G.2

**Schedule**

Block schedule: 1 1/2 sessions

Single-period schedule: 3 sessions

### Focus

_____ Activity, *TWE* p. 532

### Teach

_____ Pocket Labs, *SE* pp. 534, 539

_____ Using a Calculator, *SE* p. 535

_____ Quick Demos, *TWE* pp. 531, 536

_____ Physics Journal, *TWE* pp. 533, 537

_____ Tech Prep, *TWE* p. 534

_____ Demonstration 23-1, *TWE* pp. 538–539

_____ Connections to Biology, *TWE* p. 540

_____ Transparencies 39, 40 Masters and Worksheets, pp. 83–85, 87–88, *TCR*

_____ *Physics Lab and Pocket Lab Worksheets*, pp. 125–126, *TCR*

_____ *Laboratory Manual*, Labs 23.1, 23.2, *TCR*

_____ *Spanish Resources*, *TCR*

### Assess/Reteach

_____ Section Review, *SE* p. 541

_____ Checking for Understanding, *TWE* p. 541

_____ Reteaching, *TWE* p. 541

_____ *Study Guide*, pp. 133–136, *TCR*

_____ *Supplemental Problems*, *TCR*

### Enrichment/Application

_____ Cultural Diversity, *TWE* p. 537

_____ Extension, *TWE* p. 541

_____ *Enrichment*, pp. 45–46, *TCR*

### Close

_____ Activity, *TWE* p. 541

### Chapter Assessment

_____ Assessment, *TWE* p. 540

_____ *Alternate Assessment in the Science Classroom*

_____ *Performance Assessment in the Science Classroom*

### Multimedia Options

_____ **CD-ROM:** Electricity, *PCA*

_____ **Videotape:** *MindJogger Videoquizzes*

_____ **Videotape:** *The Mechanical Universe*, Quad 5

_____ **Videodisc:** *STVS* Chemistry, Disc 2, Side 2, Ch. 8

_____ **Software:** *Computer Test Bank*

# 23.2 Lesson Plans

## Applications of Circuits

### Section Objectives

_____ **Explain** how fuses, circuit breakers, and ground-fault interrupters protect household wiring.

_____ **State** the important characteristics of voltmeters and ammeters, and **explain** how each is used in circuits.

**National Science Content Standards** UCP.1, UCP.2, UCP.3, UCP.5; A.1, A.2, E.1, E.2, F.1, G.3

**Schedule**

Block schedule: 2 1/2 sessions

Single-period schedule: 4 sessions

### Focus

_____ Guest Speaker, *TWE* p. 542

### Teach

_____ Help Wanted, *SE* p. 543

_____ Economics Connection, *SE* p. 544

_____ Design Your Own Physics Lab, *SE* p. 545

_____ Pocket Lab, *SE* p. 547

_____ How It Works, *SE* p. 549

_____ Applying Physics, *TWE* pp. 543, 546

_____ Tech Prep, *TWE* p. 543

_____ Quick Demo, *TWE* p. 544

_____ Physics Journal, *TWE* p. 544

_____ Demonstration 23-2, *TWE* pp. 546–547

_____ Transparency 41 Master and Worksheet, pp. 89–91, *TCR*

_____ *Physics Lab and Pocket Lab Worksheets*, pp. 123–124, 127, *TCR*

_____ *Physics Skills*, Skill 19, pp. 39–40, *TCR*

_____ *Spanish Resources*, *TCR*

### Assess/Reteach

_____ Section Review, *SE* p. 548

_____ Checking for Understanding, *TWE* p. 548

_____ Reteaching, *TWE* p. 548

_____ *Study Guide*, pp. 137–138, *TCR*

_____ *Reteaching*, p. 29, *TCR*

_____ *Supplemental Problems*, *TCR*

### Enrichment/Application

_____ Enrichment, *TWE* p. 543

_____ Extension, *TWE* p. 548

_____ *Critical Thinking*, p. 30, *TCR*

_____ *Tech Prep Applications*, pp. 35–38, *TCR*

### Close

_____ Activity, *TWE* p. 548

### Chapter Assessment

_____ Chapter Review, *SE* pp. 550–553

_____ Assessment, *TWE* p. 543

_____ *Chapter Assessment*, pp. 107–110, *TCR*

_____ *Alternate Assessment in the Science Classroom*

_____ *Performance Assessment in the Science Classroom*

### Multimedia Options

_____ **Videotape:** *MindJogger Videoquizzes*

_____ **Videodisc:** *STVS* Physics, Disc 1, Side 1, Ch. 20; Disc 1, Side 2, Ch. 15

_____ **Software:** *Computer Test Bank*

# 24.1 Lesson Plans

**KEY**
*SE* = Student Edition, *TWE* = Teacher Wraparound Edition, *TCR* = Teacher Classroom Resources, *STVS* = Science and Technology Videodisc Series, *PCA* = Physics for the Computer Age

## Magnets: Permanent and Temporary

### Section Objectives

_____ **Describe** the properties of magnets and the origin of magnetism in materials.

_____ **Compare** various magnetic fields.

**National Science Content Standards** UCP.1, UCP.2, UCP.3, UCP.5; A.1, A.2, B.2, D.1, D.2, G.3

**Schedule**

Block schedule: 2 sessions

Single-period schedule: 3 sessions

### Focus

_____ Activity, *TWE* p. 556

### Teach

_____ Pocket Labs, *SE* pp. 557, 559, 564

_____ Design Your Own Physics Lab, *SE* p. 562

_____ How It Works, *SE* p. 565

_____ Quick Demos, *TWE* pp. 555, 558, 559, 560

_____ Tech Prep, *TWE* p. 559

_____ Demonstration 24-1, *TWE* pp. 560–561

_____ Physics Journal, *TWE* p. 563

_____ Connections to Biology, *TWE* p. 563

_____ Transparency 42 Master and Worksheet, pp. 93–94, *TCR*

_____ *Physics Lab and Pocket Lab Worksheets, pp. 129–133, TCR*

_____ *Laboratory Manual, Labs 24.1, 24.2, TCR*

_____ *Spanish Resources, TCR*

### Assess/Reteach

_____ Section Review, *SE* p. 566

_____ Checking for Understanding, *TWE* p. 564

_____ Reteaching, *TWE* p. 564

_____ *Study Guide, pp. 139–141, TCR*

_____ *Supplemental Problems, TCR*

### Enrichment/Application

_____ Extension, *TWE* p. 564

_____ *Enrichment, pp. 47–48, TCR*

_____ *Tech Prep Applications, pp. 39–42, TCR*

### Close

_____ Activity, *TWE* p. 566

### Chapter Assessment

_____ Assessment, *TWE* p. 558

_____ *Alternate Assessment in the Science Classroom*

_____ *Performance Assessment in the Science Classroom*

### Multimedia Options

_____ **Videotape:** *MindJogger Videoquizzes*

_____ **Videotape:** *The Mechanical Universe,* Quad 6

_____ **Software:** *Computer Test Bank*

# 24.2 Lesson Plans

**KEY**
*SE* = Student Edition, *TWE* = Teacher Wraparound Edition, *TCR* = Teacher Classroom Resources, *STVS* = Science and Technology Videodisc Series, *PCA* = Physics for the Computer Age

## Forces Caused by Magnetic Fields

### Section Objectives

_____ **Relate** magnetic induction to the direction of the force on a current-carrying wire in a magnetic field.

_____ **Solve** problems involving magnetic field strength and the forces on current-carrying wires, and on moving, charged particles in magnetic fields.

_____ **Describe** the design and operation of an electric motor.

**National Science Content Standards** UCP.1, UCP.2, UCP.3, UCP.5; A.2, B.4, E.1, E.2, F.6

**Schedule**
Block schedule: 2 sessions
Single-period schedule: 4 sessions

### Focus

_____ Activity, *TWE* p. 567

### Teach

_____ Help Wanted, *SE* p. 574
_____ Quick Demo, *TWE* p. 568
_____ Applying Physics, *TWE* p. 572
_____ Demonstration 24-2, *TWE* pp. 572–573
_____ Physics Journal, *TWE* p. 573

_____ Transparencies 42, 43 Masters and Worksheets, pp. 93–96, *TCR*
_____ *Laboratory Manual, Lab 24.3, TCR*
_____ *Spanish Resources, TCR*

### Assess/Reteach

_____ Section Review, *SE* p. 574
_____ Checking for Understanding, *TWE* p. 573
_____ Reteaching, *TWE* p. 573

_____ *Study Guide, pp. 142–144, TCR*
_____ *Reteaching, p. 30, TCR*
_____ *Supplemental Problems, TCR*

### Enrichment/Application

_____ Cultural Diversity, *TWE* p. 568
_____ Enrichment, *TWE* p. 571

_____ Extension, *TWE* p. 573
_____ *Critical Thinking, p. 31, TCR*

### Close

_____ Activity, *TWE* p. 574

### Chapter Assessment

_____ Chapter Review, *SE* pp. 575–579
_____ Assessment, *TWE* p. 569
_____ *Chapter Assessment, pp. 111–114, TCR*

_____ *Alternate Assessment in the Science Classroom*
_____ *Performance Assessment in the Science Classroom*

### Multimedia Options

_____ **CD-ROM:** Magnetic Fields, *PCA*
_____ **Videotape:** *MindJogger Videoquizzes*
_____ **Videotape:** *The Mechanical Universe,* Quad 6

_____ **Videodisc:** *STVS* Physics, Disc 1, Side 1, Ch. 20; Earth and Space, Disc 3, Side 1, Ch. 3
_____ **Software:** *Computer Test Bank*

# 25.1 Lesson Plans

**KEY**
*SE* = Student Edition, *TWE* = Teacher Wraparound Edition, *TCR* = Teacher Classroom Resources, *STVS* = Science and Technology Videodisc Series, *PCA* = Physics for the Computer Age

## Creating Electric Current from Changing Magnetic Fields

### Section Objectives

_____ **Explain** how a changing magnetic field produces an electric current.

_____ **Define** electromotive force and **solve** problems involving wires moving in a magnetic field.

_____ **Describe** how an electric generator works and how it differs from a motor.

_____ **Recognize** the difference between peak and effective voltage and current.

**National Science Content Standards** UCP.1, UCP.2, UCP.3; A.2, B.4, C.5, E.2, F.1, F.5, G.1, G.2, G.3

**Schedule**

Block schedule: 2 sessions

Single-period schedule: 3 sessions

### Focus

_____ Activity, *TWE* p. 582

### Teach

_____ History Connection, *SE* p. 583

_____ Pocket Labs, *SE* pp. 585, 588

_____ Physics & Society, *SE* p. 587

_____ Help Wanted, *SE* p. 589

_____ Quick Demos, *TWE* pp. 581, 583, 585, 586

_____ Physics Journal, *TWE* p. 584

_____ Demonstration 25-1, *TWE* p. 586

_____ Transparency 44 Master and Worksheet, pp. 97–98, *TCR*

_____ *Physics Lab and Pocket Lab Worksheets, pp. 135–138, TCR*

_____ *Spanish Resources, TCR*

### Assess/Reteach

_____ Section Review, *SE* p. 589

_____ Checking for Understanding, *TWE* p. 589

_____ Reteaching, *TWE* p. 589

_____ *Study Guide, pp. 145–148, TCR*

_____ *Supplemental Problems, TCR*

### Enrichment/Application

_____ Cultural Diversity, *TWE* p. 585

_____ Enrichment, *TWE* p. 588

_____ Extension, *TWE* p. 589

_____ *Critical Thinking, p. 32, TCR*

### Close

_____ Closing Strategy, *TWE* p. 589

### Chapter Assessment

_____ Assessment, *TWE* p. 588

_____ *Alternate Assessment in the Science Classroom*

_____ *Performance Assessment in the Science Classroom*

### Multimedia Options

_____ **CD-ROM:** Magnetic Fields, *PCA*

_____ **Videotape:** *MindJogger Videoquizzes*

_____ **Videotape:** *The Mechanical Universe,* Quad 6

_____ **Software:** *Computer Test Bank*

# 25.2 Lesson Plans

## Changing Magnetic Fields Induce *EMF*

### Section Objectives

_____ **State** Lenz's law and **explain** back-*EMF* and how it affects the operation of motors and generators.

_____ **Explain** self-inductance and how it affects circuits.

_____ **Describe** a transformer and **solve** problems involving voltage, current, and turn ratios.

**National Science Content Standards** UCP.1, UCP.2, UCP.3, UCP.4, UCP.5; A.1, A.2, B.4, B.5, E.1, E.2, G.2, G.3

**Schedule**

Block schedule: 1 1/2 sessions

Single-period schedule: 3 sessions

### Focus

_____ Discrepant Event, *TWE* p. 590

### Teach

_____ Pocket Labs, *SE* pp. 591, 593

_____ Design Your Own Physics Lab, *SE* p. 595

_____ Applying Physics, *TWE* p. 592

_____ Demonstration 25-2, *TWE* pp. 592–593

_____ Physics Journal, *TWE* p. 594

_____ Quick Demo, *TWE* p. 594

_____ Tech Prep, *TWE* p. 594

_____ Connections to Criminology, *TWE* p. 596

_____ Transparency 45 Master and Worksheet, pp. 99–100, *TCR*

_____ *Physics Lab and Pocket Lab Worksheets*, pp. 139–140, *TCR*

_____ *Laboratory Manual*, Labs 25.1, 25.2, *TCR*

_____ *Spanish Resources*, *TCR*

### Assess/Reteach

_____ Section Review, *SE* p. 597

_____ Checking for Understanding, *TWE* p. 596

_____ Reteaching, *TWE* p. 596

_____ *Study Guide*, pp. 149–150, *TCR*

_____ *Reteaching*, pp. 31–32, *TCR*

_____ *Supplemental Problems*, *TCR*

### Enrichment/Application

_____ Extension, *TWE* p. 596

_____ *Enrichment*, pp. 49–50, *TCR*

### Close

_____ Activity, *TWE* p. 597

### Chapter Assessment

_____ Chapter Review, *SE* pp. 598–601

_____ Assessment, *TWE* p. 593

_____ *Chapter Assessment*, pp. 115–118, *TCR*

_____ Alternate Assessment in the Science Classroom

_____ Performance Assessment in the Science Classroom

### Multimedia Options

_____ **Videotape:** *MindJogger Videoquizzes*

_____ **Videodisc:** *STVS* Chemistry, Disc 2, Side 2, Chs. 14, 15

_____ **Software:** *Computer Test Bank*

# 26.1 Lesson Plans

**KEY**
SE = Student Edition, TWE = Teacher Wraparound Edition, TCR = Teacher Classroom Resources, STVS = Science and Technology Videodisc Series, PCA = Physics for the Computer Age

## Interaction Between Electric and Magnetic Fields and Matter

### Section Objectives

_____ **Describe** the measurement of the charge-to-mass ratio of the electron and **solve** problems related to this measurement.

_____ **Explain** how a mass spectrometer separates ions of different masses and **solve** problems involving this instrument.

**National Science Content Standards** UCP.2, UCP.3, UCP.5; A.1, A.2, B.1, B.4, B.6, E.2, G.1, G.2, G.3

**Schedule**

Block schedule: 2 sessions

Single-period schedule: 3 sessions

### Focus

_____ Focus Strategy, *TWE* p. 605

### Teach

_____ Help Wanted, *SE* p. 605

_____ Pocket Lab, *SE* p. 607

_____ Physics Lab, *SE* p. 612

_____ Quick Demos, *TWE* pp. 603, 606

_____ Connections to History, *TWE* p. 605

_____ Connections to Chemistry, *TWE* p. 610

_____ Physics Journal, *TWE* p. 608

_____ Demonstration 26-1, *TWE* pp. 608–609

_____ Applying Physics, *TWE* p. 609

_____ Transparencies 46, 47 Masters and Worksheets, pp.101–104, *TCR*

_____ *Physics Lab and Pocket Lab Worksheets*, pp. 141–143, *TCR*

_____ *Laboratory Manual*, Lab 26.1, *TCR*

_____ *Spanish Resources, TCR*

### Assess/Reteach

_____ Section Review, *SE* p. 611

_____ Checking for Understanding, *TWE* p. 610

_____ Reteaching, *TWE* p. 610

_____ *Study Guide*, pp. 151–153, *TCR*

_____ *Supplemental Problems, TCR*

### Enrichment/Application

_____ Enrichment, *TWE* p. 608

_____ Extension, *TWE* p. 610

### Close

_____ Quick Demo, *TWE* p. 611

### Chapter Assessment

_____ Assessment, *TWE* p. 606

_____ *Alternate Assessment in the Science Classroom*

_____ *Performance Assessment in the Science Classroom*

### Multimedia Options

_____ **Videotape:** *MindJogger Videoquizzes*

_____ **Videodisc:** *STVS* Earth and Space, Disc 3, Side 1, Ch. 9

_____ **Software:** *Computer Test Bank*

# 26.2 Lesson Plans

**KEY**
*SE* = Student Edition, *TWE* = Teacher Wraparound Edition, *TCR* = Teacher Classroom Resources, *STVS* = Science and Technology Videodisc Series, *PCA* = Physics for the Computer Age

## Electric and Magnetic Fields in Space

### Section Objectives

_____ **Describe** how electric and magnetic fields can produce more electric and magnetic fields.

_____ **Explain** how accelerated charges produce electromagnetic waves.

_____ **Explain** the process by which electromagnetic waves are detected.

**National Science Content Standards** UCP.2, UCP.3, UCP.5; B.6, C.5, E.1, E.2, G.1, G.3

**Schedule**

Block schedule: 1 session

Single-period schedule: 2 sessions

### Focus

_____ Discrepant Event, *TWE* p. 613

### Teach

_____ Pocket Labs, *SE* pp. 614, 617

_____ How It Works, *SE* p. 618

_____ Quick Demos, *TWE* pp. 614, 615

_____ Applying Physics, *TWE* p. 616

_____ Demonstration 26-2, *TWE* pp. 616–617

_____ Tech Prep, *TWE* p. 616

_____ Physics Journal, *TWE* p. 619

_____ Connections to Biology, *TWE* p. 619

_____ Transparency 48 Master and Worksheet, pp. 105–106, *TCR*

_____ *Physics Lab and Pocket Lab Worksheets*, pp. 144–145, *TCR*

_____ *Spanish Resources, TCR*

### Assess/Reteach

_____ Section Review, *SE* p. 620

_____ Checking for Understanding, *TWE* p. 620

_____ Reteaching, *TWE* p. 620

_____ *Study Guide*, pp. 154–156, *TCR*

_____ *Reteaching*, p. 33, *TCR*

_____ *Supplemental Problems, TCR*

### Enrichment/Application

_____ Cultural Diversity, *TWE* p. 615

_____ Extension, *TWE* p. 620

_____ *Enrichment*, pp. 51–52, *TCR*

_____ *Critical Thinking*, p. 33, *TCR*

_____ *Tech Prep Applications*, pp. 43–46, *TCR*

### Close

_____ Closing Strategy, *TWE* p. 620

### Chapter Assessment

_____ Chapter Review, *SE* pp. 621–623

_____ Assessment, *TWE* p. 615

_____ *Chapter Assessment*, pp. 119–122, *TCR*

_____ *Alternate Assessment in the Science Classroom*

_____ *Performance Assessment in the Science Classroom*

### Multimedia Options

_____ CD-ROM: Magnetic Fields, *PCA*

_____ Videotape: *MindJogger Videoquizzes*

_____ Videotape: *The Mechanical Universe*, Quad 6

_____ **Videodisc:** *STVS* Physics, Disc 1, Side 1, Chs. 9, 19; Disc 1, Side 2, Ch. 21; Earth and Space, Disc 3, Side 1, Ch. 10

_____ **Software:** *Computer Test Bank*

# 27.1 Lesson Plans

## Waves Behave Like Particles

### Section Objectives

_____ **Describe** the spectrum emitted by a hot body and **explain** the basic theory that underlies the emission of hot-body radiation.

_____ **Explain** the photoelectric effect and **recognize** that quantum theory can explain it, whereas the wave theory cannot.

_____ **Explain** the Compton effect and **describe** it in terms of the momentum and energy of the photon.

_____ **Describe** experiments that demonstrate the particle-like properties of electromagnetic radiation.

**National Science Content Standards** UCP.2, UCP.3; A.1, A.2, B.1, B.6, E.1, E.2, G.1, G.2, G.3

**Schedule**

Block schedule: optional lesson

Single-period schedule: 2 sessions

### Focus

_____ Activity, *TWE* p. 626

### Teach

_____ Pocket Labs, *SE* pp. 627, 630

_____ Physics Lab, *SE* p. 634

_____ Sociology Connection, *SE* p. 628

_____ Help Wanted, *SE* p. 629

_____ Connections to Chemistry, *TWE* p. 627

_____ Applying Physics, *TWE* p. 628

_____ Demonstration 27-1, *TWE* pp. 628–629

_____ Quick Demos, *TWE* pp. 625, 628

_____ Physics Journal, *TWE* pp. 629, 635

_____ Tech Prep, *TWE* p. 632

_____ Transparency 49 Master and Worksheet, pp. 107–108, *TCR*

_____ *Physics Lab and Pocket Lab Worksheets*, pp. 147–150, *TCR*

_____ *Laboratory Manual*, Labs 27.1, 27.2, *TCR*

_____ *Spanish Resources*, *TCR*

### Assess/Reteach

_____ Section Review, *SE* p. 636

_____ Checking for Understanding, *TWE* p. 635

_____ Reteaching, *TWE* p. 636

_____ *Study Guide*, pp. 157–161, *TCR*

_____ *Reteaching*, pp. 34–35, *TCR*

_____ *Critical Thinking*, p. 34, *TCR*

_____ *Supplemental Problems*, *TCR*

### Enrichment/Application

_____ Cultural Diversity, *TWE* p. 631

_____ Enrichment, *TWE* p. 631

_____ Extension, *TWE* p. 636

### Close

_____ Closing Strategy, *TWE* p. 636

### Chapter Assessment

_____ Assessment, *TWE* p. 629, 630, 631

_____ *Performance Assessment in the Science Classroom*

### Multimedia Options

_____ **CD-ROM:** Quantum Theory, *PCA*

_____ **Videotape:** *MindJogger Videoquizzes*

_____ **Videodisc:** *STVS* Chemistry, Disc 2, Side 1,

Ch. 4; Disc 2, Side 2, Ch. 7; Physics, Disc 1, Side 1, Ch. 11

_____ **Software:** *Computer Test Bank*

# 27.2 Lesson Plans

**KEY**
*SE* = Student Edition, *TWE* = Teacher Wraparound Edition, *TCR* = Teacher Classroom Resources, *STVS* = Science and Technology Videodisc Series, *PCA* = Physics for the Computer Age

## Particles Behave Like Waves

### Section Objectives

_____ **Describe** evidence of the wave nature of matter and **solve** problems relating wavelength to particle momentum.

_____ **Recognize** the dual nature of both waves and particles and the importance of the Heisenberg uncertainty principle.

**National Science Content Standards** UCP.2, UCP.3; A.2, B.4, E.2, G.1, G.2, G.3

**Schedule**

Block schedule: optional lesson

Single-period schedule: 3 sessions

### Focus

_____ Convergent Question, *TWE* p. 637

### Teach

_____ Physics & Technology, *SE* p. 639

_____ Demonstration 27-2, *TWE* p. 638

_____ Physics Journal, *TWE* p. 638

_____ Quick Demo, *TWE* p. 640

_____ Spanish Resources, *TCR*

### Assess/Reteach

_____ Section Review, *SE* p. 640

_____ Checking for Understanding, *TWE* p. 640

_____ Reteaching, *TWE* p. 640

_____ Study Guide, p. 162, *TCR*

_____ Supplemental Problems, *TCR*

### Enrichment/Application

_____ Enrichment, *TWE* p. 637

_____ Extension, *TWE* p. 640

_____ Enrichment, p. 53, *TCR*

### Close

_____ Closing Strategy, *TWE* p. 640

### Chapter Assessment

_____ Chapter Review, *SE* pp. 641–643

_____ Assessment, *TWE* p. 638

_____ Chapter Assessment, pp. 123–126, *TCR*

_____ Alternate Assessment in the Science Classroom

_____ Performance Assessment in the Science Classroom

### Multimedia Options

_____ **Videotape:** *MindJogger Videoquizzes*

_____ **Videotape:** *The Mechanical Universe*, Quad 7

_____ **Software:** *Computer Test Bank*

# 28.1 Lesson Plans

## The Bohr Model of the Atom

### Section Objectives

_____ **Explain** the structure of the atom.

_____ **Distinguish** continuous spectra from line spectra.

_____ **Contrast** emission and absorption spectra.

_____ **Solve** problems using the orbital radius and energy-level equations.

**National Science Content Standards** UCP.1, UCP.2, UCP.3; A.1, A.2, B.1, B.6, D.3, D.4, G.1, G.2, G.3

**Schedule**

Block schedule: optional lesson

Single-period schedule: 3 sessions

### Focus

_____ Discrepant Event, *TWE* p. 646

### Teach

_____ Pocket Lab, *SE* p. 652

_____ Physics Lab, *SE* p. 656

_____ Quick Demos, *TWE* pp. 645, 647, 651

_____ Applying Physics, *TWE* p. 649

_____ Connections to Astronomy, *TWE* p. 649

_____ Physics Journal, *TWE* pp. 650, 654

_____ Demonstration 28-1, *TWE* pp. 652–653

_____ Transparencies 50, 51 Masters and Worksheets, pp. 109–112, *TCR*

_____ Physics Lab and Pocket Lab Worksheets, pp. 151–153, *TCR*

_____ Laboratory Manual, Lab 28.1, *TCR*

_____ Spanish Resources, *TCR*

### Assess/Reteach

_____ Section Review, *SE* p. 657

_____ Checking for Understanding, *TWE* p. 655

_____ Reteaching, *TWE* p. 655

_____ Study Guide, pp. 163–165, *TCR*

_____ Reteaching, p. 36, *TCR*

_____ Supplemental Problems, *TCR*

### Enrichment/Application

_____ Enrichment, *TWE* p. 649

_____ Cultural Diversity, *TWE* p. 650

_____ Extension, *TWE* p. 655

_____ Critical Thinking, p. 35, *TCR*

_____ Enrichment, pp. 55–56, *TCR*

### Close

_____ Activity, *TWE* p. 657

### Chapter Assessment

_____ Assessment, *TWE* pp. 649, 652, 653

_____ Alternate Assessment in the Science Classroom

_____ Performance Assessment in the Science Classroom

### Multimedia Options

_____ **Videotape:** *MindJogger Videoquizzes*

_____ **Videotape:** *The Mechanical Universe*, Quad 7

_____ **Software:** *Computer Test Bank*

_____ **Videodisc:** *STVS* Physics, Disc 1, Side 1, Chs. 13, 14, 15, 20; Disc 2, Side 1, Ch. 4

Date _____ Period _____ Name _____

**KEY**
*SE* = Student Edition, *TWE* = Teacher Wraparound Edition, *TCR* = Teacher Classroom Resources, *STVS* = Science and Technology Videodisc Series, *PCA* = Physics for the Computer Age

# 28.2 Lesson Plans

## The Quantum Model of the Atom

### Section Objectives
_____ **Describe** the shortcomings of the Bohr model of the atom.
_____ **Describe** the quantum model of the atom.
_____ **Explain** how a laser works and **describe** the properties of laser light.

**National Science Content Standards** UCP.2, UCP.3, UCP.5; B.1, B.6, E.1, E.2, F.6, G.1, G.2, G.3
**Schedule**
Block schedule: optional lesson
Single-period schedule: 3 sessions

### Focus
_____ Focus Activity, *TWE* p. 658

### Teach
_____ Pocket Labs, *SE* pp. 659, 661
_____ Help Wanted, *SE* p. 662
_____ Physics & Technology, *SE* p. 663
_____ Quick Demos, *TWE* pp. 659, 660
_____ Physics Journal, *TWE* p. 661
_____ Demonstration 28-2, *TWE* p. 662

_____ Transparency 52 Master and Worksheet, pp. 113–115, *TCR*
_____ *Physics Lab and Pocket Lab Worksheets, pp. 154–155, TCR*
_____ *Laboratory Manual, Lab 28.2, TCR*
_____ *Spanish Resources, TCR*

### Assess/Reteach
_____ Section Review, *SE* p. 664
_____ Checking for Understanding, *TWE* p. 664
_____ Reteaching, *TWE* p. 664

_____ *Study Guide, pp. 166–168, TCR*
_____ *Supplemental Problems, TCR*

### Enrichment/Application
_____ Tech Prep, *TWE* p. 661

_____ Extension, *TWE* p. 664

### Close
_____ Closing Strategy, *TWE* p. 664

### Chapter Assessment
_____ Chapter Review, *SE* pp. 665–667
_____ Assessment, *TWE* pp. 660, 661
_____ *Chapter Assessment, pp. 127–130, TCR*

_____ *Alternate Assessment in the Science Classroom*
_____ *Performance Assessment in the Science Classroom*

### Multimedia Options
_____ **CD-ROM:** Diffraction and Interference of Light, *PCA*
_____ **Videotape:** *MindJogger Videoquizzes*

_____ **Videodisc:** *STVS* Physics, Disc 1, Side 1, Ch. 16; Disc 1, Side 2, Ch. 11; Chemistry, Disc 2, Side 2, Ch. 7
_____ **Software:** *Computer Test Bank*

# 29.1 Lesson Plans

## Conduction in Solids

### Section Objectives

_____ **Describe** electron motion in conductors and semiconductors.

_____ **Compare** and **contrast** *n*-type and *p*-type semiconductors.

**National Science Content Standards** UCP.1, UCP.2, UCP.3, UCP.5; A.2, B.1, B.2, B.6, E.1, E.2, G.2

**Schedule**

Block schedule: optional lesson

Single-period schedule: 2 sessions

### Focus

_____ Discrepant Event, *TWE* p. 670

### Teach

_____ Help Wanted, *SE* p. 673

_____ Pocket Lab, *SE* p. 675

_____ Quick Demos, *TWE* pp. 669, 676

_____ Physics Journal, *TWE* p. 671

_____ Demonstration 29-1, *TWE* pp. 676–677

_____ Transparency 53 Master and Worksheet, pp. 117–118, *TCR*

_____ *Physics Lab and Pocket Lab Worksheets*, p. 159, *TCR*

_____ *Laboratory Manual*, Lab 29.1, *TCR*

_____ *Spanish Resources*, *TCR*

### Assess/Reteach

_____ Section Review, *SE* p. 678

_____ Checking for Understanding, *TWE* p. 677

_____ Reteaching, *TWE* p. 677

_____ *Study Guide*, pp. 169–172, *TCR*

_____ *Supplemental Problems*, *TCR*

### Enrichment/Application

_____ Enrichment, *TWE* pp. 672, 676

_____ Cultural Diversity, *TWE* p. 672

_____ Extension, *TWE* p. 678

_____ *Enrichment*, pp. 57–58, *TCR*

### Close

_____ Activity, *TWE* p. 678

### Chapter Assessment

_____ Assessment, *TWE* p. 673

_____ *Alternate Assessment in the Science Classroom*

_____ *Performance Assessment in the Science Classroom*

### Multimedia Options

_____ **Videotape:** *MindJogger Videoquizzes*

_____ **Software:** *Computer Test Bank*

# 29.2 Lesson Plans

**KEY**
*SE* = Student Edition, *TWE* = Teacher Wraparound Edition, *TCR* = Teacher Classroom Resources, *STVS* = Science and Technology Videodisc Series, *PCA* = Physics for the Computer Age

## Electronic Devices

### Section Objectives

_____ **Describe** how diodes limit current to motion in only one direction.

_____ **Explain** how a transistor can amplify or increase voltage changes.

**National Science Content Standards** UCP.1, UCP.2, UCP.3, UCP.5; A.1, A.2, B.1, B.2, B.6, E.1, E.2, F.6, G.1

**Schedule**

Block schedule: optional lesson

Single-period schedule: 3 sessions

### Focus

_____ Discrepant Event, *TWE* p. 679

### Teach

_____ Pocket Lab, *SE* p. 682

_____ Physics & Society, *SE* p. 683

_____ Physics Lab, *SE* p. 684

_____ Fine Arts Connection, *SE* p. 686

_____ Physics Journal, *TWE* p. 679

_____ Demonstration 29-2, *TWE* pp. 680–681

_____ Tech Prep, *TWE* p. 680

_____ Applying Physics, *TWE* p. 681

_____ Quick Demo, *TWE* p. 682

_____ Connections to Chemistry, *TWE* p. 685

_____ *Physics Lab and Pocket Lab Worksheets, pp. 157–158, 160, TCR*

_____ *Laboratory Manual, Lab 29.2, TCR*

_____ *Spanish Resources, TCR*

### Assess/Reteach

_____ Section Review, *SE* p. 686

_____ Checking for Understanding, *TWE* p. 686

_____ Reteaching, *TWE* p. 686

_____ *Study Guide, pp. 173–174, TCR*

_____ *Reteaching, p. 37, TCR*

_____ *Supplemental Problems, TCR*

### Enrichment/Application

_____ Extension, *TWE* p. 686

_____ *Critical Thinking, p. 36, TCR*

### Close

_____ Closing Strategy, *TWE* p. 686

### Chapter Assessment

_____ Chapter Review, *SE* pp. 687–689

_____ Assessment, *TWE* p. 682

_____ *Chapter Assessment, pp. 131–134, TCR*

_____ *Alternate Assessment in the Science Classroom*

_____ *Performance Assessment in the Science Classroom*

### Multimedia Options

_____ **Videotape:** *MindJogger Videoquizzes*

_____ **Videodisc:** *STVS Physics,* Disc 1, Side 1, Ch. 19; Disc 1, Side 2, Chs. 2, 14–17, 19

_____ **Software:** *Computer Test Bank*

# 30.1 Lesson Plans

## Radioactivity

### Section Objectives

_____ **Determine** the number of neutrons and protons in nuclides.

_____ **Describe** three forms of radioactive decay and **solve** nuclear equations.

_____ **Define** half-life and **calculate** the amount of material and its activity remaining after a given number of half-lives.

**National Science Content Standards** UCP.2, UCP.3; A.1, A.2, B.1, B.2, B.6, G.1, G.3

**Schedule**

Block schedule: optional lesson
Single-period schedule: 3 sessions

### Focus

_____ Focus Strategy, *TWE* p. 692

### Teach

_____ Help Wanted, *SE* p. 694

_____ Pocket Lab, *SE* p. 698

_____ Physics Lab, *SE* p. 700

_____ Quick Demos, *TWE* pp. 691, 697

_____ Demonstration 30-1, *TWE* pp. 694–695

_____ Physics Journal, *TWE* p. 696

_____ Connections to Chemistry, *TWE* p. 698

_____ Transparency 54 Master and Worksheet, pp. 119–120, *TCR*

_____ *Physics Lab and Pocket Lab Worksheets*, pp. 161–163, *TCR*

_____ *Laboratory Manual*, Lab 30.1, *TCR*

_____ *Spanish Resources*, *TCR*

### Assess/Reteach

_____ Section Review, *SE* p. 699

_____ Checking for Understanding, *TWE* p. 699

_____ Reteaching, *TWE* p. 699

_____ *Study Guide*, pp. 175–177, *TCR*

_____ *Supplemental Problems*, *TCR*

### Enrichment/Application

_____ Tech Prep, *TWE* p. 696

_____ Extension, *TWE* p. 699

_____ *Critical Thinking*, p. 37, *TCR*

_____ *Enrichment*, pp. 59–60, *TCR*

### Close

_____ Closing Strategy, *TWE* p. 699

### Chapter Assessment

_____ Assessment, *TWE* p. 695

_____ *Alternate Assessment in the Science Classroom*

_____ *Performance Assessment in the Science Classroom*

### Multimedia Options

_____ **Videotape:** *MindJogger Videoquizzes*

_____ **Videodisc:** *STVS* Chemistry, Disc 2, Side 2, Chs. 3–7; Physics, Disc 1, Side 1, Ch. 21

_____ **Software:** *Computer Test Bank*

# 30.2 Lesson Plans

## The Building Blocks of Matter

### Section Objectives

_____ **Describe** the operation of particle detectors and particle accelerators.

_____ **Define** antiparticles and **calculate** the energy of $\gamma$ rays emitted when particles and their antiparticles annihilate one another.

_____ **Describe** the quark and lepton model of matter and **explain** the role of force carriers.

**National Science Content Standards** UCP.1, UCP.2, UCP.5; B.1, B.5, B.6, D.4, E.1, E.2, F.1, G.1, G.3

**Schedule**

Block schedule: optional lesson

Single-period schedule: 3 sessions

### Focus

_____ Focus Strategy, *TWE* p. 701

### Teach

_____ Pocket Lab, *SE* p. 706

_____ How It Works, *SE* p. 709

_____ Literature Connection, *SE* p. 711

_____ Quick Demo, *TWE* p. 702

_____ Applying Physics, *TWE* p. 703

_____ Demonstration 30-2, *TWE* pp. 704–705

_____ Physics Journal, *TWE* p. 706

_____ Transparencies 55, 56 Masters and Worksheets, pp. 121–124, *TCR*

_____ *Physics Lab and Pocket Lab Worksheets, p. 164, TCR*

_____ *Spanish Resources, TCR*

### Assess/Reteach

_____ Section Review, *SE* p. 712

_____ Checking for Understanding, *TWE* p. 711

_____ Reteaching, *TWE* p. 712

_____ *Study Guide, pp. 178–180, TCR*

_____ *Reteaching, pp. 38–39, TCR*

_____ *Supplemental Problems, TCR*

### Enrichment/Application

_____ Enrichment, *TWE* p. 705

_____ Project, *TWE* p. 707

_____ Cultural Diversity, *TWE* p. 711

_____ Extension, *TWE* p. 712

_____ *Tech Prep Applications, pp. 45–48, TCR*

### Close

_____ Convergent Question, *TWE* p. 712

### Chapter Assessment

_____ Chapter Review, *SE* pp. 713–715

_____ Assessment, *TWE* p. 708

_____ *Chapter Assessment, pp. 135–140, TCR*

_____ *Alternate Assessment in the Science Classroom*

_____ *Performance Assessment in the Science Classroom*

### Multimedia Options

_____ **Videotape:** *MindJogger Videoquizzes*

_____ **Videotape:** *The Mechanical Universe*, Quad 2

_____ **Videodisc:** *STVS Physics, Disc 1, Side 1, Ch. 20*

_____ **Software:** *Computer Test Bank*

**KEY**
*SE* = Student Edition, *TWE* = Teacher Wraparound Edition, *TCR* = Teacher Classroom Resources, *STVS* = Science and Technology Videodisc Series, *PCA* = Physics for the Computer Age

# 31.1 Lesson Plans

## Holding the Nucleus Together

### Section Objectives

_____ **Define** binding energy of the nucleus.
_____ **Relate** the energy released in a nuclear reaction to the change in binding energy during the reaction.

**National Science Content Standards** UCP.1, UCP.2, UCP.3; A.2, B.1, B.2, B.4, B.5, B.6, D.4, G.2

**Schedule**
Block schedule: optional lesson
Single-period schedule: 2 sessions

### Focus

_____ Focus Strategy, *TWE* p. 718

### Teach

_____ Pocket Lab, *SE* p. 719
_____ Help Wanted, *SE* p. 721
_____ Quick Demos, *TWE* pp. 717, 721
_____ Demonstration 31-1, *TWE* pp. 718–719
_____ *Graphing Calculators in the Science Classroom*

_____ *Physics Lab and Pocket Lab Worksheets, p. 167, TCR*
_____ *Laboratory Manual, Lab 31.1, TCR*
_____ *Spanish Resources, TCR*

### Assess/Reteach

_____ Section Review, *SE* p. 721
_____ Checking for Understanding, *TWE* p. 721
_____ Reteaching, *TWE* p. 721

_____ *Study Guide, pp. 181–182, TCR*
_____ *Supplemental Problems, TCR*

### Enrichment/Application

_____ Extension, *TWE* p. 721

### Close

_____ Closing Strategy, *TWE* p. 721

### Chapter Assessment

_____ Assessment, *TWE* p. 720
_____ *Alternate Assessment in the Science Classroom*

_____ *Performance Assessment in the Science Classroom*

### Multimedia Options

_____ **Videotape:** *MindJogger Videoquizzes*
_____ **Videotape:** *The Mechanical Universe*, Quad 7

_____ **Videodisc:** *STVS* Chemistry, Disc 2, Side 2, Ch. 3
_____ **Software:** *Computer Test Bank*

# 31.2 Lesson Plans

**KEY**
*SE* = Student Edition, *TWE* = Teacher Wraparound Edition, *TCR* = Teacher Classroom Resources, *STVS* = Science and Technology Videodisc Series, *PCA* = Physics for the Computer Age

## Using Nuclear Energy

### Section Objectives

_____ **Define** how radioactive isotopes can be artificially produced and used.

_____ **Solve** nuclear equations.

_____ **Define** *nuclear fission* and *chain reaction*.

_____ **Describe** the operation of one or more types of nuclear reactors.

_____ **Describe** the fusion process.

**National Science Content Standards** UCP.1, UCP.2, UCP.3, UCP.5; A.1, A.2, B.1, B.5, B.6, C.1, C.5, D.3, D.4, E.1, E.2, F.1, F.4, F.5, F.6, G.1, G.2, G.3

**Schedule**

Block schedule: optional lesson

Single-period schedule: 4 sessions

### Focus

_____ Focus Strategy, *TWE* p. 722

### Teach

_____ Physics Lab, *SE* p. 727

_____ Pocket Lab, *SE* p. 728

_____ Physics & Technology, *SE* p. 732

_____ Applying Physics, *TWE* p. 723

_____ Tech Prep, *TWE* p. 723

_____ Quick Demo, *TWE* p. 725

_____ Demonstration 31-2, *TWE* p. 726

_____ Physics Journal, *TWE* pp. 729, 730

_____ Connections to Astronomy, *TWE* p. 731

_____ Transparency 57 Master and Worksheet, pp. 125–126, *TCR*

_____ *Physics Lab and Pocket Lab Worksheets, pp. 165–166, 168, TCR*

_____ *Spanish Resources, TCR*

### Assess/Reteach

_____ Section Review, *SE* p. 732

_____ Checking for Understanding, *TWE* p. 730

_____ Reteaching, *TWE* p. 731

_____ *Study Guide, pp. 183–186, TCR*

_____ *Reteaching, p. 40, TCR*

_____ *Supplemental Problems, TCR*

### Enrichment/Application

_____ Cultural Diversity, *TWE* pp. 723, 728

_____ Enrichment, *TWE* pp. 725, 728

_____ Extension, *TWE* p. 731

_____ *Critical Thinking, p. 38, TCR*

_____ *Enrichment, p. 61, TCR*

### Close

_____ Activity, *TWE* p. 732

### Chapter Assessment

_____ Chapter Review, *SE* pp. 733–735

_____ Assessment, *TWE* pp. 724, 725, 730

_____ *Chapter Assessment, pp. 141–144, TCR*

_____ *Alternate Assessment in the Science Classroom*

_____ *Performance Assessment in the Science Classroom*

### Multimedia Options

_____ **Videotape:** *MindJogger Videoquizzes*

_____ **Videodisc:** *STVS* Chemistry, Disc 2, Side 2, Chs., 4, 6, 7; Earth and Space, Disc 3, Side 2,

Ch. 19; Physics Disc 1, Side 1, Ch. 21; Disc 1, Side 2, Ch. 12

_____ **Software:** *Computer Test Bank*

# Notes

# Notes